W9-BCT-879

THE ECONOMICS OF EDUCATION:

CONCEPTUAL PROBLEMS AND POLICY ISSUES

THE ECONOMICS OF EDUCATION: CONCEPTUAL PROBLEMS AND POLICY ISSUES

RICHARD PERLMAN
Professor of Economics
University of Wisconsin-Milwaukee

83955

McGraw-Hill Book Company

*New York   St. Louis   San Francisco   Düsseldorf   Johannesburg
Kuala Lumpur   London   Mexico   Montreal   New Delhi   Panama
Rio de Janeiro   Singapore   Sydney   Toronto*

The Economics of Education: Conceptual Problems and Policy Issues

1 2 3 4 5 6 7 8 9 0 BPBP 7 9 8 7 6 5 4 3

This book was set in Press Roman by Textart Service, Inc.
The editors were Jack R. Crutchfield and Edwin Hanson;
the cover designer was Pedro A. Noa; and the production supervisor was Joan M. Oppenheimer.
The printer and binder was The Book Press, Inc.

Library of Congress Cataloging in Publication Data

Perlman, Richard.
    The economics of education.

    1. Education—Economic aspects—United States.
I. Title.
LC66.P47   338.4'3   73–3363
ISBN 0-07-049305-7

For Irma

CONTENTS

vii

PART II POLICY ISSUES

PREFACE

Although consideration of man as a human resource with an economic value that can be measured in dollars and cents can trace its origins to Adam Smith and before, it is only for the past twenty years that the subject has become an important area of economic study. This brief book discusses the conceptual problems of measurement and policy issues associated with investment in education, probably the most important contributor to the resource value of man, that is, to his human capital.

The individual gains more than higher earnings from his schooling, and society nets additional benefits from the education of its members, apart from increased production. Neither, though, should ignore economic factors in educational decision making. Benefits flow from prior costs, and the relationship between costs and returns plays its part in deciding whether investment in schooling is superior to alternative uses of limited private and public funds.

Unfortunately, these costs and returns associated with schooling are difficult to calculate, even the measurable ones, to say nothing of imponderable factors. This book details the conceptual difficulties and weaknesses in estimating the size and direction of economic influences on educational investment decisions. It ends up in the middle ground, concluding that cost-benefit, or rate-of-return, analysis provides a faulty economic guide to the investor, but taking the pragmatic stand that, being the best we have, it should be used, albeit cautiously, in formulating policy in the increasingly important area of educational investment.

At the same time public concern over the economic wisdom of expanding educational outlay has increased, with the focus on greater investment efficiency; so too has our preoccupation with the means of financing schooling, with special reference to widening educational opportunity, in the cause of equity. Financial policy issues and programs for altering our present system for funding early and higher education close this brief glimpse of important economic aspects of education.

Not only the economics or education student who wishes a fuller treatment of the economics of education but the "intelligent reader" as well—he of strong mind and will who has so far refrained from formal study of economics—should find this book's indirect, time-and-mental-effort costs low. Direct, our-of-pocket costs are also nominal. Whether it pays to buy and read the book depends on the importance the reader attaches to a clearer understanding of the human capital concept applied to education and on how well the book serves this purpose. The writer does not dare suggest that consumption benefits associated with the joy of good reading will also arise.

In their examination of problems and issues, these pages recount and review the works of many contributors to the field. By disclaiming theoretical originality for hiw own effort, the writer makes uninhibited use of their ideas, their insights, and their research findings.

RICHARD PERLMAN

THE ECONOMICS OF EDUCATION:
CONCEPTUAL PROBLEMS AND POLICY ISSUES

CHAPTER ONE

Introduction

We readily accept the fact that one man earns more than another, whether earnings are measured by hourly wage, weekly salary, or annual income. In fact, we attribute these earnings differences to differential contributions to the value of production. In short, we accept the principle that the worker is worth his hire, and we even slip into the easy explanation that "a man is paid more because he is worth more."

But this expression is used only as a shortened form of the wordier conclusion that one man is paid more than another because the market value of his services is greater. There is no judgment implied about their relative worth as human beings in describing one man as a $120-a-week clerk and another as a $50,000-a-year executive.

When differences in earnings streams are expressed as asset values, something is lost in translation. The same public opinion that accepts the notion that one man is worth $25 an hour and another $3 rejects the notion that one man has a value of $200,000 and another $25,000. Who would place an economic value on a human being, so the charge goes, except a Philistine, or worse, an economist? In fact, though, there is no more need to confuse the human investment value of a man with his value as a human being than there is in confusing a person's "net worth," a term we accept without qualm, with his worth as a person.

To some, putting a price on a man brings back shades of slavery. But the economist does not want to compare the intrinsic worth of a man to that of a machine, nor does he wish to put mankind on the block to be sold to the highest bidder. His only purpose in *capitalizing* earning streams, that is, finding the present value of a succession of future earnings, is for comparison with the present value of other money streams that differ in their timing and magnitude.

THE NEED FOR HUMAN CAPITAL EVALUATION

When the need arises, we do put prices on individuals, or even on parts of the body. Compensation schedules for work-related injuries set different values for the loss of a left arm, a right eye, a whole life. Negligence suits make awards in lump-sum present payments based on the expected future earning power of the injured person and the extent to which that earning power is impaired. Breach of promise and alienation of affection suits imply that even the heart has its price. But the study of human capital would indeed be a trivial science if its only applications were to peripheral legal matters.

Capitalization permits monetary evaluation of measures designed to raise a man's economic worth. More precisely, it facilitates measurement of returns to investment in man and aids in the decisions on whether given human investments should be undertaken.

With no other investment in him than in the maintenance of his health, the mature man is economically similar to unimproved land that has been protected from destruction by fire and erosion. His future earning power, and current asset value, with no past investment in his education, training, or development of his skills, is limited to the productivity of his native endowments of strength, quickness, and industry. To raise his economic value, man must be developed as a human resource. Investments must be made in him to increase his future earning power. Chief among these investments are those in his schooling and training.

The human capital approach measures the added returns of these investments against their costs. Here the economist and humanist part company. The latter decries the dollar measurement of the benefits from, say, a college education. To him the psychic benefits to the individual of the broadened perspectives and refined and expanded tastes and activities that learning and knowledge bring defy quantification. Furthermore, he fears that if the economist's calculations show the economic returns to a certain educational program fall short of their costs, the student might thereby be deterred from acquiring the learning in question and lose all its nonmonetary benefits.

The economist does not share this concern. He argues that the economic aspect is just one of many to be weighed in making a long-term decision involving the expenditure of much time and money. The economist knows that other considerations may outweigh the economic effects in human investment choices, but he would at least like to provide the prospective students and government bodies who finance education with information, imperfect though it may be, on the economic costs and benefits of the investment outlays. He expects that they will use this information, weigh it, and perhaps have it outweighed by noneconomic factors.

In the long-past halcyon days of education when college was for the gilded youth and professors as a class were independently wealthy, learning and teaching were carried on well isolated from the pressures of society and the exigencies of the market. Then college curricula and goals were designed for enlightening the mind and elevating the spirit. There was no question of investment for the purpose of raising later earning power. Now, though, since college has reached out to more millions, with enrollment increasing from under 4 million to above 8 million, or about 40 percent of college-age youths, over the decade of the 1960s, many students show great interest in the economic aspects of their education. The cost in time and money is far too great for them to undertake these expenses without regard to ensuing economic benefits. While the typical student may still consider the nonmonetary returns from college important, he would like to know the monetary pluses and minuses to make a rational decision on how much education he can afford.

The same changes have occurred in public decisions on higher education. When public colleges were few and often poorly supported, the slight budgetary strain involved did not induce much interest in financial comparison of social returns with taxpayer costs. But now with total public higher educational expenditures rising rapidly from $8.8 billion to $14.6 billion over the brief four-year span 1965-1969 and with public college enrollment more than doubling during the 1960s,[1] there is growing skepticism of whether such great outlays are worth the money.

---

[1] Elchanan Cohn, *The Economics of Education*, Heath, 1972. This work contains a wealth of data on finance, enrollment, and many other aspects of education.

For a time, showing a good deal of cultural lag, state and local colleges proliferated, and tax money was spent without much question or inhibition. Education by its very nature was assumed worth the cost. But eventually elements of scarcity, so dear to the heart of the economist, began to be felt. Education outlays, at all levels, primary and secondary as well as college, began to compete for the tax dollar with other worthwhile needs. Priorities began to change. Twenty years ago even considering deferral of a new school to allow sewer system improvements would have raised community eyebrows. Today, those who hold the civic purse could opt for the sewers without feeling the least bit anti-intellectual.

In state and local budgets, education is following the path of the military in the federal budget, moving from unquestioning acceptance of authorization requests to demand for greater efficiency in spending tax dollars (trimming the fat) to serious doubts about the need for such a high basic-expenditure level (shrinking the body). Neither can any longer claim essentiality as justification for unlimited outlays. Both are in danger of falling from the status of sacred cows to budgetary pariahs.

The point may be a bit exaggerated, but surely there is growing interest in the economic side of costly measures that improve and expand our knowledge, as well as concomitantly strengthen our earning power. In fact, perhaps unknowingly, we have always made human investment decisions based on economic factors. For example, in the health field, consider as important a thing as the life-span. We could probably lengthen our lives a little if we underwent daily complete physical checkups.

Why is this rarely or never done? In the first place there are the money costs of the examination. But we can even neglect these by holding that life itself is so important to us that we would undergo any reasonable money expense to lengthen it. On the same grounds, we can even ignore any lost income from time spent on the checkups. Even if money were not a factor, we would still reject the opportunity to lengthen our lives in this manner. Subjectively, we value the benefit of, say, five minutes extra life less than the discomfort (cost) of two hours of waiting and examination.

This decision is no less economic than if dollars and cents were involved. Economics deals with choice among alternatives in a world of scarcity, and economists recognize time, along with money, as one of life's limited essentials. Surely most of us would give up much time and money to lengthen our lives. But the economist is trained to think in terms of incremental or marginal changes and adjustments, and the above example explains that some point would be reached when we would no longer trade some of our economic resources and current time for extra time at the end of life.

The humanist is joined by the humanitarian in opposing economic study of human investment projects. What is the rate of return on investment in a nursing home? The costs are high and the returns, measured by the future earnings of the aged patients, zero. Does this simple calculation not expose economics as truly the "dismal science"? But a nursing home does not even fit the economist's concept of an investment, defined as an asset that adds to the earning power of the holder. Public funds are not spent on the aged ill in order to restore them to work, but these expenditures are like those on parks and playgrounds—outlays that satisfy community consumption goals.

The economist knows that nursing homes provide valuable care for the aged even if this care leads to no economic returns in added production from its recipients. He also knows what the aged value most—a listening ear, companionship, attention from their indifferent middle-aged children—are both costless and priceless.

But there is some legitimate economic interest in cost-benefit analysis of nursing homes, even if the benefits themselves are not quantifiable. The nursing home must compete with dollars spent on other public consumption goods. Priorities must be established among them for equal money outlays. There is also economic concern over the efficiency of the home's management. The most services should be secured for every dollar spent, and to the extent efficient management can reduce total cost, these savings might push the home ahead of other projects in the community budget. In any case, although the home provides worthwhile services in the care and treatment of the aged, sentiment is poor justification for inefficiency.

The social reformer adds his criticism of monetary examination of human investments. Suppose the goal is to raise the education level of blacks. Suppose further that because of past unequal schooling it is found that a given quantity of college money spent would be more successful in raising the educational attainment and achievement of the previously more favored whites. Then would the economist not conclude that on efficiency grounds the money spent on scholarships, low-interest loans, grants-in-aid, etc., should be placed on whites where the results would be more pronounced, even if this policy widened the racial educational differential contrary to the original social goal of equalization?

Why should he? The economist does not respect economic efficiency in the abstract as more important than the pursuit of social policy. He would want the money spent most efficiently *to attain the policy goal*. But once he was satisfied on this matter, he would only want to estimate the cost of the program in order to compare its priority rating with that of other social goals, given their importance and costs.

Consider a related racial issue of more pressing immediacy. Suppose the goal is for improved race relations, and the consensus view holds that the best way to reach this nebulous but laudable end is through school integration by busing, with racial intermingling beginning in the innocent years of early childhood. The economist will work under the assumption that purposeful racial mixing of schools would improve race relations. That is, he will try, heroically, to place dollar values on costs and benefits of busing.

The sides for and against busing base their arguments, again, on efficiency considerations. That is, they try to support a social viewpoint by economic reasoning which, interestingly enough, an economist would not use. The issue seems to center on whether the quality of education, for white or black children or both, would improve or suffer because of busing. The social reformer argues that the data show better educational results with busing; the supporters of the status quo and the segregationist cite other data which show a deterioration in schooling results, but the economist does not consider the effects on educational quality as necessarily crucial in judging the wisdom of the practice.

If the effect on education were favorable, the economist would be as happy as the next person that a social goal had been attained at a negative cost. He would not be much discouraged, though, by unfavorable findings. He knows that repairing the damage of discrimination will be costly, whether the form is educational support, housing subsidy, low-cost business loans, or income maintenance guarantees. The economist considers negative educational effects from forced school integration as only a partial determinant of the merit of the program.

He is well aware that parents are touchy about their children's welfare, so that negative educational effects might outweigh any other considerations, but still he would like to judge all aspects of the issue. Are there better means to achieve racial harmony that involve a lower social cost? Are there somewhat less effective means which cost much less than a slightly reduced quality of education? If the answer to both questions were negative, then the economist would have provided information in support of the program. To maintain that findings of negative educational benefits to any extent, no matter how slight, would make adoption of busing against society's interest, would assume, contrary to the basic premise, a zero social value for improved race relations.

But the problem is not that simple, and the economist's contribution not that definite. For one thing, sociologists and psychologists may debate whether closer contacts between groups lead to understanding. Even assuming, though, that the benefits for racial harmony of busing were definite, the economist's "information" on costs is not. Translating possible adverse schooling effects into later earnings differences—the means of assigning dollar value to these effects can only yield rough estimates with a wide range for error and uncertainty, perhaps wide enough to provide "economic" support for either side of the busing issue.

Thus, while we have argued against the humanistic, humanitarian, and societal view that there is something misleading, destructive, or even faintly indecent about studying the economic aspects of investment in man and suggesting that dollars-and-cents estimates of costs and returns should actually play an important part in these investment decisions, critics of the human capital approach are on firmer ground when they question the accuracy of the calculations rather than their morality.[2] Although the need for economic information on educational costs and benefits is great, unfortunately economic analysis can but imperfectly satisfy this need. On the issue of the value of this faulted information of the human capital approach to educational decisions, the following pages come down heavily in the middle. Weakened by methodological difficulties as the economic signals from this approach may be, used cautiously, they can guide private and public education policies toward the optimal allocation of the limited economic resources of time and money. In any case, they are the best signals we have.

---

[2] Of course, the terms "investment" and "human capital" imply that expenditures on people, which will have long-run effects such as education and health, are designed to increase the earning power of the recipients. But the preceding argument, aimed at explaining the value and importance of economic study of these expenditures, does not require terminological bias in its defense.

HUMAN AND PHYSICAL CAPITAL COMPARED

The expression "man is not a machine" can serve as more than a philosophical outcry against the application of capital theory to humans. It can be used against the economist on his own grounds.

In fact, labor economics itself constitutes a separate subdiscipline simply because people are neither machines nor commodities. Workers do not necessarily supply their services to the highest bidder because they also value working conditions, chances for promotion, job location, etc., as well as wages. Similarly, the individual worker, unlike the firm, cannot have income maximization as his goal; a 168-hour work week can be very tiring. He does try to maximize his satisfaction, or utility, from the allocation of his time, which he divides between income-generating work and leisure. But when objective measurement by dollars-and-cents calculations are modified to allow for subjective concepts like satisfaction or utility, behavioral predictions lose precision to the cause of realism.

In short, labor market analysis is complicated by the fact that work is done by people who cannot separate themselves from the services they render and who therefore must expend time and effort in providing these services. These complications also enter into the employer's labor policy. He must be concerned with labor relations, with the morale and motivations of his work force. Firms try very hard to have good personnel relations departments; needless to say, not a penny is spent on machine relations.

These same immeasurable elements prevent pat conclusions regarding the merit of investment projects in man. Individuals do not decide whether schooling "pays" solely on monetary considerations. They are interested in resulting changes in their lives as well as in the rate of return on their investment in education. Similarly, public decisions on educational investment are influenced by indirect results from the projects—the effect on economic growth and societal changes, for examples.

While it is convenient and not very unrealistic to hold that business steadfastly pursues profit maximization or, in the case at issue, the highest returns on its investment, it is impossible to conceive of a fixed optimization goal for individuals and society in their educational investment decisions. When utility and welfare enter as factors, and especially if the importance of these factors changes over time, straightforward calculations of dollar costs and returns and rates of return leave much to be desired as guides to private or social educational investment policy.

For example, if education contributes to economic growth and society considers growth important, government investments in education would seem appropriate even if calculated rates of return on these investments were low relative to those on other investments less stimulating to growth. But this long-run decision may prove unwise (uneconomic) because of our changing attitudes toward growth, which, as a matter of fact, because of environmental side effects is actually losing popularity as a social goal.

It might be argued that business also faces uncertainty—about tastes, market shifts, technological changes, etc.—in its current investment decisions that must judge a distant future. But the physical capital investor does not have to worry about a fundamental change within his optimization goal.[3]

Government decision makers could assume that current social goals are the best guides to future goals, much the same way as the forecaster in the absence of clear signals may predict that tomorrow's weather will be much like today's. But this practice would add nothing to the probability that the long-term investment decision would maximize welfare.

As an example of the uncertainty created by nonmonetary considerations in private investment decision making, an individual may prepare for an occupation for which calculated rates of return on educational investment are lower than for other fields because he prefers this type of work. But what if his tastes or preferences change in later life?

Following Lord Kelvin's view that if a thing cannot be measured it is not worth talking about, we could overlook the imponderables that bedevil decision making in the human investment—specifically education—field. But economics never claimed to be as precise a discipline as physics, and these elements are too important to ignore. It is worth trying to incorporate them in a study of the contributions of the economic cost-benefit analysis to the issues involved. There is weakness, though, in a method that tries to add subjective values to calculated ones to arrive at unequivocal results.

---

[3] Neil W. Chamberlain, "Some Second Thoughts on the Concept of Human Capital," *Proceedings of the Twentieth Annual Meeting*, Industrial Relations Research Association, 1967, stresses the importance of changing social values as a factor against the application of capital theory to social human investment decisions.

THE RATE-OF-RETURN APPROACH

Conceptual problems related to the components of the rate-of-return approach are analyzed in the next three chapters. First costs are treated (Chapter 2), then returns (Chapter 3), and finally the rate of return itself (Chapter 4)–all within the framework of conventional human capital analysis.

These three factors are discussed from the *private* and *social* point of view. Direct, measurable costs and returns differ for the two but, more specifically, so do their optimizing constraints and goals.

If calculation of rates of return is to serve as any more than an intellectual exercise, the rates should provide some aid to educational investment decision making, both for the private and public sector. In fact, the investment decisions–whether or not the student should undergo more schooling (and the analysis is limited to formal education) or whether or not the state should expand educational plant and facilities or provide direct assistance to students–are the principal policy issues to which the analysis is directed. After conceptual difficulties in calculating the rate are noted throughout the earlier chapters, uncertainties in applying the rate to the private investment decision are discussed in Chapter 5 and to the public investment decision in Chapter 6.

The last two chapters treat important current issues in educational finance. For earlier schooling there is controversy over the merits of the property tax as a basis for school funding and over the voucher plan as a substitute for our present school system (Chapter 7). In higher education there is concern over means of facilitating educational funding to widen financial opportunity for college attendance through grants, loans, equity financing, and deferred and variable payment plans. The equity of the current equal tuition subsidization for all students in public universities is under serious question (Chapter 8).

PART

I

Conceptual
Problems

CHAPTER TWO

Educational Investment Costs

To decide whether or not a particular investment "pays," in the narrowest economic sense without regard to nonmonetary benefits, rate-of-return analysis applied to the individual compares alternatives. In the specific case under discussion, the comparison is between the rate that would be realized on educational investment costs with that which would have been earned had the money been invested in physical capital. For society as a whole, the alternative investment refers to other potential governmental projects.

In either case, the alternative investment represents a foregone opportunity. Economic rationality demands that the individual's actual employment of his time and money yield greater, or at least as great, benefits as their next best use, their *opportunity cost*, whether reference is to wages of labor, satisfaction from a dollar spent on consumption, or returns to an educational investment. To the poet, the saddest words of all are "what might have been"; the calculating economic man's lamentation would be equally doleful if his opportunity costs exceeded his actual returns.

While the need for an accurate calculation of educational investment costs is great, unfortunately this information is not easily obtainable and not of the highest accuracy. It is small support to the validity of the rate-of-return approach as a whole that the conceptual problems associated with returns and the rate of return are probably even more serious than those that confound cost analysis.

COST COMPONENTS

Direct Costs

Carrying the opportunity-cost concept further, for comparison with other investments, all costs should be measured by their opportunity costs.[1] Economic analysis of investment in education has a simple two-element taxonomy for costs.

First there are the "direct costs," or out-of-pocket expenses, of tuition, books, fees, extra room-and-board expenses, and incidentals. All these for the primary and secondary students, attending public schools, are negligible, and the zero values for these costs conventionally used in rate-of-return studies do little harm to the accuracy of calculations. Of course, for college students these costs are substantial, even for the student who attends a public college with tuition heavily subsidized by state or city.

"Social direct costs" differ from the above "private" ones in that they represent the expenses incurred in providing education without regard to the payer. For rate-of-return calculations they consist of the annual costs per student of plant and equipment and of teachers and other labor, etc., employed. Obviously, direct social costs exceed private costs, especially for lower schooling levels; but even for college social costs are greater except for the special case of full-cost tuition.

Actual money outlays can be assumed to measure the opportunity cost of direct costs. If, though, for example, teachers could not earn as much in alternative employment, opportunity costs would be lower than actual out-of-pocket expenses on these salaries. But there are enough serious conceptual problems in the rate-of-return approach without chasing down minutiae to prove its weakness.

Indirect Costs

These costs are the greatest contributor to the fuzziness in total cost measurement. "Indirect costs," which are the same for private or social estimates, represent the opportunity cost of the student's time,

---

[1] This is the main theme of Fritz Machlup, *The Production and Distribution of Knowledge in the United States*, Princeton University Press, 1962, in his analysis of educational investment.

that is, his "foregone earnings" while attending school. Although no cost outlay is involved, unrealized earnings represent a heavy expense to the student. Estimates of the share of these costs to total private costs for college students run as high as 75 percent.[2]

The basic difficulty in measuring indirect costs arises from the simple fact that an individual cannot carry out alternative activities at the same time. How can we estimate the income foregone by a student who goes to college at age eighteen instead of going to work? Imprecision enters conventional cost calculations which estimate foregone earnings of college students by the average earnings during college-age years of a cohort of noncollege youth similar in age but different in so many other ways. We standardize. We try to correct for differences in family wealth, intelligence, or whatever variable we can isolate, but we can never succeed in measuring the actual money value of "what might have been."

Rough as even the adjusted earnings of noncollege youth may be, they are probably the best guide we have to the resource cost of school-work per student, from the *social* viewpoint, or the equivalent foregone earnings of *private* educational investment. As an alternative proxy for the shadow price of student labor, part-time earnings rates of working students are a poor guide to opportunity-cost measurement. The typical student takes any job that comes along that can support him and pay school expenses. Certainly, he would earn a higher wage rate at a full-time job, selected on the basis of interests and aptitudes and perhaps prior training.

Misconceptions about College Costs

Financing college costs by parents The manner of financing education affects private costs. As noted above, private direct costs for publicly financed grade schools and high schools are close to zero. Public colleges typically finance a great part, but not all, of the student's direct costs. Scholarships and fellowships help, but they are rarely large enough to provide a good substitute for foregone earnings in maintaining the student during his college years.

---

[2] Gary Becker, *Human Capital*, National Bureau of Economic Research, 1964.

In many cases parents pay not only direct college costs but living expenses as well. If private costs refer to family expenses,[3] they are unaffected by which household member finances them, even if the student's *personal* costs are reduced by parental support.

Many parents, who pay upwards of $20,000 for the college education of their children, would not give a penny toward alternative use of their time. At first view, this money might appear as an offset to college costs in that the opportunity cost of the college education would be $20,000 less. But this money would remain to the family, if not the youth, to be invested elsewhere. The money might be applied to the student's college education, either to provide him with nonmonetary consumption benefits in later life or perhaps to add to parental prestige from having college-educated children. Although either case falls outside our provisional framework of strictly monetary motivation for education, the expenses can be considered costs, with the returns taking an unquantifiable form which confounds calculation of the true rate of return. If man were a machine, this complexity would not arise. Only when parents limit their support to education for the financial returns from this investment can returns be measured.

Financing costs through student work   Many students work while going to college. If they work during the summer, the income received has no effect on college costs. Foregone earnings refer to would-be labor income for about a forty-week school year. Summer income helps defray college costs but it does not reduce them.

Students also work during the school term. Again, these off-hour earnings do not reduce the investment costs of schooling. Conceptually the working student is a moonlighter, laboring forty hours a week at school and, say, twelve hours at a paying job. If the student did not attend school, he could apply the entire fifty-two hours to paying work.

Once more a question regarding preference for educational investment arises, this time as to whether the student would be willing to work all these hours if he did not go to college, and once more the question is irrelevant to the issue of proper measurement of the opportunity cost of foregone earnings. If he would work more to derive psychic benefits from education in later life, then returns would not be

---

[3] By this convention, nongovernment scholarships and fellowships would be excluded from private cost accounting, and their receipt would reduce private costs.

quantifiable; and if he did so because of the higher later income, the returns would be measurable, but in either case the time spent in school-work could have been devoted to market earnings.

The poor student is more likely to have to work while attending school to finance his college education than is the more fortunate student of independent means. It is therefore sometimes erroneously concluded that college costs the poor student more because he must exert more effort, and thereby forego leisure to acquire his education. No one would deny that the heavy time-and-effort burden placed on the working student deters many capable youths from college attendance. But when he is sufficiently attracted to education to engage in the extra effort required to finance his schooling, his foregone leisure is rewarded by extra income. His actual schooling *costs* him no more time, effort, or foregone earnings than the student with adequate funds expends. Misconception arises from confusing the defraying of costs with the actual costs themselves.

Perhaps the difference can be made clearer by thinking of a college education as a commodity with the same price to all buyers. The demand will be lower for poor students with their lesser wealth, and those poor who buy education do so at greater sacrifice of their limited resources. In fact equalizing *financial* educational opportunity means equalizing demand schedules so that those with the same tastes and abilities would demand, and presumably obtain, the same degree of education. Means to equalize other aspects of education demand, such as ability in schoolwork, and opportunity for later use of skills acquired are another matter to be discussed in the policy chapters.

Financing costs by limiting consumption The social opportunity cost of a college education may be as high as $40,000. For the average student, private costs might be about $10,000 less, the difference resulting from the deviation from full-cost tuition, with the reduction being the highest for students at public colleges and universities. Foregone earnings, the bulk of college costs, are the same in either case.

This $30,000 to $40,000 figure is not inconsistent with the earlier statement that a parent would pay $20,000 for a child's college education, even with the implicit assumption that this lower amount would completely finance the four-year program, including living expenses as well as direct college costs.

Maintenance is one thing, and foregone earnings quite another. The college student, by adopting a different life-style, can consume much less than the earnings he foregoes by spending time at school rather than working. But college *costs* are not necessarily closely related to what the student consumes. For comparability with other uses of his time and money, the crux of rate-of-return analysis, opportunity costs not actual expenditures are the relevant cost element.

As an extreme case, the student may follow a "nuts and berries" existence and spend practically nothing in maintaining himself during his college years. No matter, his investment opportunity costs are still measured by his direct college charges and his foregone earnings. These measure the value of resources he could have derived returns from had he not gone to college. They are also society's costs of not having the resources applied to other uses. Again, the relevant issue is not the ease or difficulty in meeting the costs, but the actual costs themselves.

Financing costs by loans Some students now finance their education through loans. Undoubtedly, the trend toward this type of financing will move sharply upward, as plans to equalize financial opportunity for higher education become more fully developed. While the subject of student loans as a financing device will be analyzed in the last chapter, here we can note the effect of loan financing on educational costs.

At first view, it appears obvious that interest charges represent an education cost. This might or might not be the correct view, depending on how one treats these costs. Use of alternative rates of return on other investments to decide on the profitability of educational investment implies that the funds would be available for investment elsewhere. But if the student must borrow to finance his schooling, he does not have funds for other investments.

Thus, the interest charges on schooling loans could be treated as a cost, and if the present value of his education returns discounted by the alternative rate exceeded costs, including interest, education would "pay" as an investment. A different and more realistic treatment for the student who cannot make alternative investments which would yield the same result would simply treat the interest charges as the discount factor, with the investment decision dependent on whether discounted returns exceeded costs net of interest.

The result is unaffected by the fact that market interest rates are higher for school loans than for other interest loans. But conceptually there is a difference in that the former method would yield higher costs for the borrowing student, while the latter would leave costs unaltered but measure the added burden to the borrowing student as a higher "alternative" rate of return.

If "market rates" for student loans were no higher than the level for other borrowing, and these loans were available to all potential borrowers, then the financial burden would be the same for students who borrowed as for those who paid their own way. The main purpose of modern student loan programs is to equalize the financial burden of meeting educational costs by removing capital-market imperfections and thus reducing, or hopefully eliminating, inequality in financial educational opportunity.

COST MODIFICATIONS

While student borrowing may or may not require modification of costs, depending on the method used, there are elements in the investment process which definitely affect the cost concept. We treat four of them here. The first, "consumption benefits during schooling," may be considered minor in fact if not conception. The second, "learning while earning," applies to both private and social return estimates. The third, "compulsory education," arises because of the difference between social and private costs, while the last, "unemployment," certainly requires modification of private costs, and depending on one's outlook may or may not affect social costs.

Consumption Benefits during Schooling

All those nonmonetary advantages from education which accrue to the student such as broadened tastes and interests; more prestigious, responsible, and interesting work; increased respect from society; and an ineffable feeling of well-being are collected under the rubric of consumption benefits. While these benefits are studied as returns, consumption benefits which arise during the educational process itself affect costs. For an accurate measure of foregone earnings, we want to know what could have been earned from market work equal to that directed to school. If work has an effort as well as a time dimension and if school effort is less than market work, then the opportunity cost of schoolwork is less than foregone market earnings for the same period of time.

Undoubtedly grade school work is less arduous for the child than market labor would be. Perhaps high school work is too. But as a practical matter there is no need to modify cost estimates downward because of the consumption benefits, or lesser strain, from school effort at these levels. The rate of return on early education far exceeds that from alternative investments for society and is not even a private decision issue at all because of compulsory education during these years.

For college, though, where rates of return are not so high, the presence of consumption benefits during schooling could conceivably tip the scales in favor of schooling. The issue is not whether there are consumption benefits from college but whether these exceed those from market work during college-age years. Colleges do structure social activities—dances, football games, etc.—but the working youth is not without his social life.

As for the effort at work itself, there is no strong basis for arguing one way or the other. In fact, if we believe in the adage "man invented work to avoid thinking," schoolwork would be harder than market work, requiring an upward adjustment to the labor cost in school investment.

It is probably best simply to accept Schultz's view that "students study which is work, and this work, among other things, helps create human capital. Students are not enjoying leisure when they study. . ."[4]

---

[4] Theodore W. Schultz, "Capital Formation by Education," *Journal of Political Economy*, vol. 68, December 1960, p. 573. Schultz adds: . . . "nor are they engaged wholly in consumption; they are here viewed as 'self-employed' producers of capital." The word "wholly" would best be deleted, since it invites comparison with possible consumption benefits from market work and possible nonquantifiable modification of costs.

At this stage, by ignoring differences in consumption benefits, we avoid what Mary Jean Bowman, "The Costing of Human Resource Development," in G. E. A. Robinson and John Vaizey (eds.), *Conference on the Economics of Education*, Macmillan, 1966, p. 473, calls the "utility quagmire." Consumption benefits in later life after schooling cannot be this easily dismissed.

Learning while Earning

Some students work at jobs which relate to their later careers. For example, teaching assistants gain experience which adds to their ability as teachers in after-school life. Work as a teaching assistant constitutes an overload of effort, whether this work is added to a full school schedule or, what amounts to the same thing, stretches out the schooling period. If earnings of teaching assistants are no less than their foregone earnings for the time so employed, then whatever extra earnings they received in later life because of the experience gained just adds to the returns from their educational investment.

If, as is more likely, they earn less than they would have for other market work, then the cost of education would be higher by the difference between the two wages. The higher returns received from the extra earnings would compensate for this extra cost.

In the nonacademic field, all apprenticeship and on-the-job training programs are designed to contribute to occupational development. Characteristically, the worker receives a lower training wage than he would have earned in full-time market work if he were not a trainee. The labor cost of his training investment then is simply the difference between his earnings foregone and his actual training wage.

What has happened to the opportunity-cost aspect of educational investment costs? Why do we not count the foregone earnings as costs and the training wages as early returns? We could do so, but this artificial treatment in the cause of conceptual purity would not affect estimated rates of return.

Compulsory Education

The individual must accept society's constraints as a datum. Thus, there are no private opportunity costs of foregone earnings for children subject to compulsory education and child labor laws. If school is work, though, compulsory education is a euphemism for a type of forced child labor.

Since child labor laws prevent market work, then the only labor cost to the child is the value of his lost leisure time. In any case, it would be an academic exercise of the most impractical kind to quibble about the modification to private costs of early schooling. The rate of return on this investment is high, even with cost modifications; there is no doubt that nonmonetary benefits from early schooling are sizable, and, in any case, society has taken the question of early schooling out of the private decision-making sphere.

There is more than hair-splitting pedantry at issue over the societal, or governmental, decision to make schooling compulsory. Again, there is no question about the advantages of early schooling, but uncertainty arises over just where the age limit for compulsory attendance should be set.

Unlike the individual, society has the capacity to establish constraints, but to test the wisdom, in this case economic rationality of welfare optimization, results must be compared with those that would have been obtained had the constraints not been set. If the age of compulsory education is pushed up from sixteen to seventeen, then the indirect social cost of this move is measured by the foregone market earnings of sixteen-year-olds. Even with total compliance to the requirement, so that there would be no proxy group of sixteen-year-old workers whose earnings could be used to estimate foregone earnings, it would be illogical to consider them as zero. What others earn only serves as a proxy value for what the school group could have earned. Of course, estimating foregone earnings would require even more imagination and mystical shadow pricing than if there were a working cohort.

Thus, it would be illogical or deceitful, depending on their intelligence, for those who enacted the rise in the minimum school-leaving age to claim that the move was socially costless because school attendance prevented market work when the authorities themselves set these constraints. It does not undervalue the noneconomic aspects of educational decisions to argue that when government authorities decide that the public welfare would be improved by advancing the age for compulsory schooling without considering the consequent cost in lost output, they really have not decided anything. They have assumed a great deal.

Unemployment

While average earnings by high school graduates generally fall short of the opportunity cost of college time because of the greater average motivation, intelligence, and other income-generating attributes of college youths, in one sense they exceed foregone earnings. College is work, say 1,600 hours a year, comprised of forty 40-hour weeks. The student working at school on a fixed schedule never faces the problem of unemployment of his schooltime. The same cannot be said of the 18- to 22-year-old market worker. Presumably, the student would encounter the same employment uncertainties if he chose market instead of college work.

Assume an unemployment probability of 20 percent, a painfully high but not unrealistic figure for youths today. Conventional treatment of the effect of unemployment on opportunity costs simply counts only 80 percent of average full-time earnings of noncollege young workers as a measure of the earnings lost while attending school.

Although this method ignores the value of foregone, albeit involuntary, leisure of unemployment, it does roughly take the effect of unemployment probability on private educational investment costs into account. The individual has no control over labor market conditions and must accept the unemployment rate as a given fact.

Should the same downward cost adjustment be made for unemployment in calculating social investment costs? The question actually hinges on whether the state has any choice or control over unemployment. Most people would like to think it does, but if government policy has aimed at zero or close to zero unemployment, its record over the years has not been an outstanding one. In fact, most would agree that if the government pushed hard toward this goal, the harmful side effects of inflation would pose a social cost that would substantially, if not completely, offset the employment gain.

Certainly, local bodies—based on our past and current economic history—and the federal government itself must take some level of unemployment as a datum. For practical purposes some unknown (slowly rising) minimum level—is the target rate now 5 percent?—is beyond the government's power to reduce. Although special efforts are being made to lower the very high rate for youths, this rate has stubbornly resisted these attacks.

Therefore, arguments by some analysts that high unemployment is a short-run phenomenon while investment decisions are long-run in nature, or that we should not introduce inability of the government's monetary and fiscal policies to achieve negligible unemployment in an analysis of the economic costs and benefits of educational investments, miss the point that the effect of unemployment on social investment costs is not logically related to that of the minimum school-leaving age. The latter represents government choice regarding a social institution; the former is, in effect, out of government control, putting the government much in the same position as that of an individual in respect to established laws and customs which he must accept. In short, as far as social costs are concerned, some level of unemployment has been institutionalized outside the framework of social policy. To argue otherwise substitutes wishful thinking for a clear appraisal of long-run experience.

How unemployment is treated in measuring social costs is not an unimportant problem, and the issue warrants consideration. Assume foregone earnings at three-fourths of total college costs. Unemployment for youths has averaged close to 20 percent in recent years, but allowing for some long-run improvement and the offset of higher employability of those in school over the proxy nonstudent group, and of the slight benefit of unemployed leisure, 10 percent would represent a reasonable figure for the percentage reduction in earnings of college-age nonstudents required to approximate foregone earnings. Thus, correct treatment of unemployment reduces total costs by about 7.5 percent, an amount sizable enough in some instances to be crucial in determining whether education investment "pays" in the narrowest economic sense. Expressed in a different way, failure to acknowledge that some degree of youthful unemployment would persist despite corrective government policy might lead to a false economic signal, which heeded, would deny investment in a socially profitable educational project.

SUMMARY

While there is great need for accurate cost figures in the determination of profitability of an investment project, one can only derive imperfect cost estimates for educational investment. The difficulty appears in evaluating labor input of students. They forego earnings, but how much must always be uncertain because shadow prices must be estimated for foregone earnings. Earnings of the age-peer working group corrected for differences in ability, family income, intelligence, motivation, etc., give the best, but still inaccurate, measure of these foregone earnings.

Foregone earnings costs are unaffected by the means of financing these costs, whether from the student's own resources, from market work while attending school, from reduced consumption, or from loans. Private costs, as opposed to social costs, are reduced by scholarships and government subsidization, but as a practical matter these extra funds usually only cut into direct costs without lowering indirect costs.

Consumption benefits during schooling, if greater than those associated with market work life, would reduce educational costs, but the difference between the two is probably not great enough to worry about.

When workers learn while they earn, in some form of training program, their foregone earnings are measured by the difference between what they would have received from a regular job and their trainee wage. Presumably this shortfall will be compensated by later higher earnings.

Compulsory education eliminates foregone earnings from private costs for covered students. But an implicit value for these earnings should be included in social costs, since society has options regarding the constraints it sets.

Similarly market unemployment for college-age youths reduces private foregone earnings costs. Whether or not social costs should also be reduced is debatable. It depends on whether we consider a given level of youth unemployment beyond the government's decision-making power to influence.

All in all, the picture of investment costs is confused, if not confusing. Conceptual uncertainties and unquantifiable elements make accurate measurement impossible. Turning to study of investment returns, the search for precision becomes even more arduous.

CHAPTER THREE

Returns
To
Education

The *direct* financial returns to education are the extra earnings received in later life that can be attributed to the schooling acquired. While conceptual difficulties arise in the measurement of these returns, by far the greatest uncertainties relate to consideration of *indirect* returns, even for those which yield monetary benefits, but especially for those which add nonmonetary, nonquantifiable advantages from schooling.

The chapter begins with a discussion of the factors entering calculation of direct monetary returns, then moves to modification of those returns, and to a study of indirect monetary and nonmonetary returns, including returns not captured by the educated individual, but by society as a whole.

DIRECT FINANCIAL RETURNS

Extra Earnings from Education

The first approximation to the true earnings difference attributable to an education program, say college, conventionally totals the annual difference in average college graduate earnings and average high school graduate earnings for every year after college completion until the end of the work life. Looking ahead to rate-of-return calculations in the next chapter, these annual differences in returns will have to be discounted by a rate that will equate their present values to college investment costs in order to derive the "internal rate of return." But here we are only interested in the returns themselves.

Again, as with cost calculations, what we would really like to know, but never can, are the earnings that the typical college graduate would have realized in later life had he not gone to college. As with costs, the proxy value of high school graduate age-cohort earnings provides a faulty shadow price, or opportunity cost, to the college graduate of his would-be earnings because of differences in ability, intelligence, motivation, etc., between the two groups. In addition, later earnings are greatly influenced by family wealth, parents' earnings and education.

Attempts have been made to correct for all these methods by isolating them, and thus deriving the "pure" contribution of education to earnings. The method of multiple correlation used tends to obscure the role of education because of strong intercorrelation between the variables. For example, while the father's education seems to contribute a great deal to earnings, it also is a major determination of education; thus, the analysis which shows a weak relationship between education and earnings, in isolation, misses the effect of the father's education on earnings operating *through* the close tie between parental schooling and education.[1]

Futurity in Estimation of Returns

Relevant returns differences occur in the future, while only past and present returns are available for estimation of the future returns. If data on average annual earnings differences between college and high school graduates had been available over the past forty-five years, the approximate postcollege work life, we could calculate what the rate of return was forty-five years ago. But this value would not provide much help for college investment policy decisions today, except under the heroic assumption that these exact differences would prevail over the next forty-five years.

[1] This point is raised by M. Blaug, "The Rate of Return on Investment in Education in Great Britain," *The Manchester School*, vol. 33, 1967, reprinted in M. Blaug (ed.), *Economics of Education I*, Penguin, 1968.

Similarly, conventional use of current age-cohort earnings differences may be far off the mark as a representation of future earnings differences. For example, if forty-two-year-old college graduates average $3,000 more per year today than high school graduates of the same age, by what logic, except for the need of working with some value, can we state that twenty-four years from now—the time when those making the college investment decision today will be forty-two—this earnings difference, relevant for calculating *today's* rate of return, will be the same $3,000?

In defense of human investment analysis, it can be argued that physical investment decisions face the same uncertainty about future returns, and business decision makers, while acknowledging imprecision in their forecasts, do not give up in despair but try to base decisions on probabilities and intelligent, or experienced, guesses. But the problem of futurity of the elements in returns is different in degree, if not in kind, between the two investments.

The sought-after rate of return on business investment, assuming random errors in forecasting future returns, is most affected by near-term earnings on the investment. The discounting process reduces the contribution of distant earnings to the capitalized present value of total future earnings. Since firms can make close estimates of earnings in the near future, then the uncertainty of later futurity has little effect on estimated rates of return.

But for educational investment, a systematic bias may arise that affects all future earnings at the *same rate*, thus making contributions to the present value of returns in the distant unforseeable future just as important as the more predictable near-term returns. If wages are tied to productivity and productivity increases uniformly for high school and college graduates over time, say 3 percent a year, then the *absolute* earnings difference will rise by the same percentage each year, making discounted future net earnings from education for the most distant year as important a contributor to the present value of returns as next year's difference.

Thus, apart from other uncertain factors that affect the estimate of future returns, an educated guess must be made regarding the productivity or growth element. The effect of secular growth on the earnings differential between high school and college graduates may have a crucial effect on the rate of return. Becker calculates about 1 percent change in the calculated rate for each 1 percent difference in the estimated growth rate.[2]

MODIFICATION OF DIRECT RETURNS

Unemployment

Once more, correction must be made for unemployment effects. In later work years, the high school educated worker is more likely to suffer unemployment than the college graduate. Again, to measure the time effect of unemployment, the edge should be taken off actual rates because of the slight benefits of free time associated with involuntary idleness.

Unemployment differences generate two conflicting forces on returns. On the one hand the higher rate for the lesser educated tends to widen the returns to education, but then the higher earnings level of the educated suffers a greater absolute offset for the adjustment to any given unemployment level. For example, if in a given future year the average college graduate were to earn $12,000 and the high school graduate $6,000, and the expected unemployment rates were 5 percent and 8 percent, respectively—and the correct values for future unemployment is anybody's guess—the unadjusted earnings difference of $6,000 would shrink to $5,880 (0.95 × $12,000 − 0.92 × $6,000) after adjustment for unemployment.

In this example, the higher income of the college-educated worker outweighed the effect of a lower unemployment rate in leading to an adjusted differential lower than the level before unemployment was considered. Adjustment has no effect on the raw differential in the special case of equal and opposite income and unemployment ratios.

What was debated about inclusion of an adjustment factor for unemployment in calculating social costs also applies to social returns. Adjustment should be made if a given rate of unemployment, different for different educational attainment levels, is considered outside public economic policy to affect.

[2] Gary Becker, *Human Capital*, National Bureau of Economic Research, 1964, pp. 73-78.

The very process of increased education, though, may help reduce the unemployment level. If structural imbalance—job openings but unemployed workers unqualified to fill them—is an important contributor to unemployment, then expansion of education and training would lower the institutionalized unemployment rate.

In any case, whether private or social returns are considered the mitigating factor on the adjustment of higher earnings *levels* of the more educated reduces the actual amount of the adjustment, and the practical importance of the conceptual problem at issue.

Mortality

We do not live forever, and many who make the decision whether or not to invest in college at age eighteen die before the end of their work life. The adjustment for mortality is similar to that for unemployment. Average annual earnings for both the college and high school groups at every age should be multiplied by the probability of living to that age. Since the early and middle work years contribute most to the (discounted) present value of annual returns, and death rates are very low for these years, the mortality correction is a small one, and fairly closely predictable.

The effect of the mortality adjustment reduces net returns because life-span is not significantly related to educational attainment, and a more or less equal *percentage* reduction in earnings for each group results in a lowered *absolute* earnings differential.

The mortality adjustment is the same for social returns. Society has little or no option regarding the life-span.

Taxes

To calculate private (net) returns, earnings should be considered net of taxes since the monetary gain to the individual is measured by his disposable income. That higher taxes contribute to the general welfare does not add any differential benefit to the payer's economic condition, nor do tax expenditures particularly benefit high over low payers.

The effect of the income tax adjustment is to lower private net returns; more taxes are paid by the educated because of both their greater earnings and the progression in the tax rate. For estimating social returns, though, taxes should not be deducted. Presumably, all income taxes are used for the benefit of society as a whole. Thus society gains not only from the higher earnings of the educated, which at this stage of the analysis we equate with greater production as a result of schooling, but in addition from the public goods and services which their higher taxes buy.

INDIRECT MONETARY BENEFITS

On-the-Job Training

There appears to be a definite positive relationship between the amount of formal education and on-the-job company training received.[3] Investment which a firm makes in the training of a worker becomes embodied in him no less than the educational investment he purchases himself, no matter that the human investments financed by a particular firm are usually directed to the development of skills of specific value to the firm itself. In fact, firms tend to invest more in workers the more schooling they have because these workers can add to their productivity more easily (cheaply) from having specific training grafted on to their knowledge acquired through formal schooling.

Earnings are higher for those who have company training added to their schooling investment. Although the company may contribute all training investment costs, as a practical matter it cannot keep all the returns. To give the worker incentive to undergo training, even if the training can only be applied to the firm's particular output, the company will pay him more than his opportunity cost.

But the higher earnings attributable to training are subsumed in returns to schooling. It might seem incorrect to attribute extra earnings to education that in fact result from on-the-job training. The conceptual issue here is whether the returns to a given level of schooling

---

[3] This is the finding of Jacob Mincer, "On-the-Job Training: Costs, Returns, and Some Implications," *Journal of Political Economy*, vol. 70, October 1962, Supplement.

should be reduced to the extent that later higher earnings are attributable to postschooling training received, rather than to the schooling itself.

Since training is dependent on education, there is logic in the conventional method of including the returns from training as part of the monetary returns to education. Then, though, it might seem that this procedure commits the classic error in calculation of double counting; extra earnings of the training are counted as returns to education and certainly as returns to training.

Reference to the effect of changing time horizons on investment calculations defends the logic of counting the returns twice. Suppose an eighteen-year-old student invests in college training as a biologist. His education leads to an income received from routine laboratory work with a drug concern that exceeds the earnings he would have received from a different job had he not gone to college. This earnings difference measures returns to his education. Now, though, if the firm decides to spend money training him as a pharmaceutical salesman, grafting other skills onto his biological knowledge, his added income will serve as the appropriate earnings from which to measure his returns to education. The new net earnings stream will be discounted to age eighteen.

Assume that he is offered this opportunity for company sales training at age twenty-four. The decision is an easy one for him to make at that time, assuming his interest in selling is at worst no weaker than in laboratory work. With the company paying for everything, down to a training wage equal to his current salary, the worker has zero investment costs and will therefore receive an infinite rate of return on any subsequent earnings above his current level.

Thus, counting the returns on training twice does not represent double counting in the usual sense of the term. The returns are counted twice but from different time horizons related to the distinct investment decisions made by the same individual. In his first decision, at age eighteen, the student expects returns as a laboratory technician and later higher net earnings as a salesman. He should modify these latter earnings by the degree of uncertainty that he will follow the path from laboratory to on-the-job training and selling. In his second decision, at age twenty-four, he takes advantage of further income-raising investment that costs him nothing. In short, his college education provides him with a valuable option to receive on-the-job training as a salesman.

Option Value of Education

Similarly, every early and intermediate stage of education provides the student with the option to continue to the next level.[4] This option has an economic value provided that the rate of return at each higher level exceeds that on alternative investments.

Just as in the case of estimating the value of the option of a degree in biology that allows for sales training, calculating the returns on any higher educational levels twice does not involve double counting. The returns from high school to a fourteen-year-old include the option value of his high school diploma to attend and profit from college and postcollege education. The returns from college to an eighteen-year-old, or to the same youth four years later, are simply those he will realize on his college investment, and whatever option value his degree has to earn additional returns on still further educational investment.

Unlike options on physical property, the right to further education has no market value. It cannot be sold or traded. Nevertheless it does have economic value to the prospective investor in education. The value of the option is based on the probability that it will be exercised. As such, its value varies from individual to individual. Thus, another variable is added to the list of those that influence the economic basis of educational investment decisions.

This option value applies only to intermediate educational levels. If we were to calculate the returns on the further education of a fourteen-year-old who goes through college, then, of course, the option value of his high school diploma becomes incorporated in his returns to college and is not to be calculated separately.

Effect of education on work-force productivity If we assume the smooth working of a competitive capitalistic economy, in which workers are paid the value of their marginal product, the extra earnings attributable to education will measure the productivity gains of those receiving the education. In Chapter 6 we will discuss the complications that arise when wages are not tied to productivity. Nevertheless, the high returns of the educated to a large degree reflect their increased productivity resulting from schooling.

---

[4] Burton Weisbrod, "Education and Investment in Human Capital," *Journal of Political Economy*, October 1962, introduces and analyzes the financial option values of education.

This is not a very profound observation. Although man is not a machine, if education is an investment, in effect, it provides extra tools for the worker that accompany his labor effort. The income from these acquired skills are the nonlabor part of his earnings, his returns on educational investment. But to carry the analogy of human capital to tools further, the educated worker's human capital is often used to raise the production of his coworkers as well, just as a machine aids the productivity of many workers. Of course, human investment is more personalized than physical capital, and most of the improvement in productivity is confined to the recipient of the investment. But an educated worker can, for example, improve production techniques, modify office procedures, and in many ways raise efficiency of other workers.

To the extent he does this, private returns will in fact be reduced since the consequent rise in earning power of the lesser educated resulting from their productivity gain will narrow average earnings differentials between groups at different educational levels. Correction should be made in calculating the social returns to add the productivity-related earnings gain of the lesser educated who profit from the greater total investment, in this case the human investment in the educated.

This correction is easier said than done. We seek, but can never really find, the would-have-been earnings level for the lesser educated had their productivity and earnings not been raised by the increase in capital consequent to the human investment in the educated.

In two senses of the term these added social returns from increased productivity of other workers can be considered an externality; they are indirect by-products of education and their benefits are not captured by the education recipient. But in our later treatment, externalities will be confined to those elements which do not raise monetary returns.

Miscellaneous Indirect Monetary Benefits

Weisbrod discusses many forms of indirect monetary benefits from education—a few of them noted here—which accrue both to the individual and to society as a whole.[5]

---

[5] Weisbrod, *op. cit.* For an extensive analysis of Weisbrod's examples see Martin O'Donoghue, *Economic Dimensions in Education*, Aldine, 1971.

Child-care services At least for the early years of schooling, apart from their instructional efforts, teachers also provide parents high-quality free child-care services. Parents can go about their business or play with probably even less worry than if their children were cared for in the home.

This service provides benefits to the individual parent and therefore contributes to private as well as social returns, if we extend the meaning of private returns to include those received by the investment recipient's household as well as by himself. Their value could be treated as an offset to costs rather than as returns since the part of school expenses that in effect pays for the teacher's supervision and not for her instruction are not really investment costs of education. As returns they free the parent's time, especially that of the mother, for valued leisure—under the realistic assumption that she can find more satisfying use of her nonmarket time than child care for the school period—or for gainful employment.

Although the dollar value of these auxiliary teacher services total a substantial amount, they have but slight importance for social policy decisions. As has been repeatedly stressed, the noneconomic benefits (essentiality) of early education provide enough basis for the policy of universal coverage without the need for superfluous support of high economic returns. At later ages, when the economic returns to education are less certain, so too are the value of teacher's child-care services. At sixteen or seventeen, school supervision is not needed to protect the youth from danger, and there is no evident tendency for enforced schooling to keep him out of mischief.

Generational transmission of education All studies indicate a tendency for the children of highly educated parents to reach a high level of schooling themselves. This generational transmission of educational attainment may result from any of several causes—inherited aptitude for schooling, effective home instruction that raises the child's chances for school success, a predilection for schooling instilled in the child, and high income of the parent that permits easy school financing. Whatever the source, as long as the rate of return on higher educational investment exceeds that on alternative uses of capital funds, a gain to the individual results from the educational investment that takes place. Society also gains as education is expanded, if total returns from educational investment exceed those on equal alternative investments. Then positive social economic gains follow from an expansion of investment, in this case transmitted by parental guidance, encouragement, and support, That is, children of educated parents are more likely to have better information about the higher returns from education and better opportunity to take advantage of them. Individual differences in information and opportunity and higher returns imply that the market for schooling is less than perfect.

Do-it-yourself educational by-products Individuals derive additional returns from education and training through application of their schooling to homework or do-it-yourself projects. The plumber or carpenter could make most of his own home repairs; the average taxpayer could make out his own return. For these simple but important tasks, the social gain, being the sum of all private implicit earnings from self-service effort, forms a substantial addition to total returns.

When the taxpayer calculates his own taxes, he deprives a tax accountant or consultant of a client. Considering current or past returns, an implied reduction in tax-expert income should not be made. Estimated net returns on their schooling reflect actual earnings, which are lower than they would have been had they served more taxpayers. An additional deduction to their lost income would represent an egregious example of double counting. The gain to the taxpayer of the imputed value of these services, with the qualifying offset of the value of leisure foregone, etc., are real enough, though, and should be counted as a secondary return to his schooling, which gave him the ability to do his own tax work.

But what if there is a future extension in literacy, or, to give an even more pointed example, what if high schools give a course in "taxpayer education"? Then it might seem that the social gain of indirect financial benefits of self-filing by taxpayers will be offset by the social loss of reduced income or even unemployment among tax experts. Such, though, is not the case.

The immediate blow to the tax consultant business of new courses in taxpayer training may be severe, but in the long run labor will be diverted from this rapidly narrowing field. To argue that the isolated depression in these occupations will become chronic or even permanent is to speak little of the economic rationality of occupational choice among the coming generations. The same weak argument—and unfortunately it has all too often been raised—could be made against any technological advance. When machines replace men, jobs are initially lost but are regained in the long run, as productivity gains raise real income and total demand for goods and services.

Recall that above, in admitting that relevant social returns are long run in nature, it was still held that a certain significant level of overall unemployment should be counted in estimation of foregone earnings during schooling and in all earnings afterwards, in calculating even the social rate of return. The above discounting of particular unemployment resulting from what amounts to a productivity gain for the educated creates no inconsistency. Assuming that our historical economic drag of significant unemployment will continue indefinitely does not deny that the economy will grow and demand expand in response to productivity gains—a response that in effect keeps our unfortunate, but nevertheless characteristic, unemployment rate from rising.

To press the issue further, though, there is some question whether there are any *social* economic returns from individual tax filing. To argue that there are may require circular reasoning. To some extent, we have complex tax forms *because* our people are well educated. But society has an option regarding the type of taxes imposed and the manner of collection. With a less-educated society, we could levy taxes which required much less individual reasoning power to calculate.

NONMONETARY RETURNS—CONSUMPTION BENEFITS

In this and the following section we treat those added benefits from education which, though difficult and sometimes impossible to quantify, are nevertheless real contributions to the individual and society. They must be considered in individual and societal decision making and may be of crucial importance when calculated rates of return on educational investment are close to or below the expected rate on alternative investments. Does it not reveal the weakness of the whole approach to admit that ultimately, after careful statistical analysis of all measured and estimated variables, decisions may be based on elements that are both imponderable and subjective? But these pages only offer lukewarm support to the rate-of-return, or cost-benefit, approach to educational decision making in describing it as the best available.

Consumption benefits, treated here, yield private and perhaps social returns. Externalities, discussed in the next section, benefit society as a whole.

Consumption benefits should not be confused with consumption expenditures. These are the outlays by nonbusiness units (households) for goods and services, which may or may not give pleasure, even though they serve a useful function. Take the case of our food purchases. All are listed as consumption expenses, but considering man as a human resource, the outlay for calories and nutrients count as maintenance costs; all else is for consumption benefits. The sauces and seasoning, even the knives and forks and napkins, everything beyond basic alimentation are the expenses we incur to differentiate dining from gorging, to provide consumption benefits from eating.

In the health field, a gall bladder operation is both investment (repair) and consumption expense. In that it permits a longer life, the investment aspects refer to the lengthened period of earnings, and consumption benefits result from the increased opportunity of more and more comfortable, work-free time on earth. The cosmetic effects of plastic surgery nose realignment give only consumption benefits.

When consumption expenses are unrelated to the development or maintenance of man as a human resource, expenses and benefits come closer together. We go bowling for the fun of it, and the expense provides its benefits. What if we have to wait for an hour for an alley? This might be a very unenjoyable use of nonwork time, but further analysis of the varying benefits of time would take us too far afield.

We place consumption benefits from education into two classes, "leisure-related" and "work-related benefits." To some degree they are interrelated. Whatever job satisfaction the educated worker enjoys, this feeling of well-being at work carries over to off-work hours. To garble poetry a bit, "Investment to the physical capitalist is a thing apart, 'tis the human capitalist's whole existence."

One consumption benefit from education which applies to both work and leisure may be called the "stigma-prestige effect" of college. This effect cuts across all uses of time, work and play, coloring the individual's whole life. Years ago a college education was a source of prestige. It suggested the intelligence, ambition, foresight, and right (conventional) values associated with those who attain a privileged status. Now, quite the contrary, with about half our population continuing education after high school, not to go to college is fast becoming a sign of mental weakness, poor parental guidance, wrong values, and insensitivity to public attitudes. We are told repeatedly that "you can't get anywhere without a college education." No matter that rate-of-return studies show that you don't get much further with one. Whether there is prestige in going or stigma in not going to college, this effect adds a psychological consumption benefit for college-educated workers compared to those whose educations stops short of this level.

Leisure-related Consumption Benefits

The fact that purely "leisure-related" consumption benefits associated with college raise returns on college education is much less certain. What really matters in this area is the comparison of satisfactions derived from leisure-time use of the college and high school graduate. Interpersonal comparisons of utility are difficult to make, and the welfare economist usually avoids the issue by only considering an unequivocal gain in total utility those changes which add to the utility of one person without reducing that of another.

Similarly, for the same individual, education alters and modifies tastes. It may also widen them. The college graduate, in effect, becomes a different person with respect to his pleasures and tastes. But to the extent that he enjoys both fine wine and beer, foreign travel and picnics, concerts and television, his choice for consumption satisfaction expands. The gain in economic terms arising from this wider option for free-time pleasures lies in the ability to raise the (equal) marginal utility from time and money spread out among a variety of activities, rather than concentrated in just a few.

Only in cases in which tastes are so changed that the simple pleasures of the uneducated no longer satisfy the college graduate is the question of greater consumption benefits from college in doubt. Only the intellectual snob would argue that a good opera lifts the spirit more than a hard-hitting prizefight. More to the point, it is by no means certain that the college graduate finds the opera a more satisfying experience than the prizefight he would have enjoyed had he not gone to college. We are not arguing here that ignorance is necessarily bliss, but that foregone pleasures, lost in the preference-changing process of education, might be stronger than the new ones acquired. In the absence of any data or even logical presumption in one direction or the other, expedience suggests that we consider that the taste-changing aspects of education have a neutral, or zero, effect on individual consumption benefits.

Work-related Consumption Benefits

Studies indicate a pronounced tendency for the higher educated to work more in later life.[6] This extra time at work takes the form of more years in the work force, on average, and in the absence of data showing a contrary tendency for annual hours worked, extra years can be translated into extra time worked on an annual basis. Some correction seems in order for this greater work participation. Returns from a human investment should reflect the greater earning power resulting from the investment. At first view, then, if the individual recipient of the investment decides to earn more by working more, this added income is attributable to the extra labor effort and not to the investment. Consequently, net returns should be reduced by the earnings of the extra work time of the educated.

While data on the nature of the individual labor supply schedule are by no means conclusive, they indicate a tendency toward a negative response of work effort to an increase in earnings rates. Here we have a puzzling contradiction. How can we explain the greater labor supply of the college trained, who also enjoy higher earnings rates than the lesser educated?

The college graduate may work longer hours because he finds his work stimulating and its responsibilities challenging. He takes pleasure in the importance and prestige of his position.

---

[6]William G. Bowen and T. Aldrich Finegan, "Labor Force Participation and Unemployment," Arthur Ross (ed.), *Employment Policy and the Labor Market*, University of California Press, 1965, and the same authors, "Educational Attainment and Labor Force Participation," *American Economic Review*, Papers and Proceedings, vol. 56, May 1966, find labor force participation rates rise with the level of education.

The gain from education is conceptually clear even if it cannot be easily measured. If the disutility of work time weighs less heavily on the college-educated man, even at the same earnings rate, he would choose to work more hours than if he held a "high school graduate" job, since at the margin the cost to him of an hour's market time would be less. Measured in effort units, which are more inclusive than time units in that they include the unpleasantness of an hour's work as well as the time spent, the college graduate can supply more time to the market with the same effort than if he had been forced to work at the less satisfying jobs to which a lesser education would limit him.

As a practical matter, then, the fact that if the educated work longer hours because of their greater satisfaction or, more realistically, their lesser disutility from the jobs they hold, makes for correct use of annual differences in earnings as the measure of returns to education; no downward adjustment in returns is required for the greater work time of the educated.[7]

A different type of response to work-related consumption benefits does tend to underestimate returns from education. Certain jobs, held by educated workers, because of their prestige, independence, or absence of stress and strain, pay less than others. Adam Smith noted this phenomenon in his discussion of compensating differences of inequalities in wages among jobs requiring the same preparation. Certainly, work-related consumption benefits count as returns to the individuals holding these favored jobs. In fact, it is their attraction which swells the number seeking them, driving earnings from them down.

In analyzing these income-reducing, work-related consumption benefits, Bowen mulls over the issue whether they should be counted among *social* returns.[8] On the one hand, Bowen, following Smith in pointing out the tendency for lower rates of pay for the most satisfying jobs at each skill or required education level, is inclined not to adjust social

[7]In their detailed rate-of-return study, James Morgan and Martin David, "Education and Income," *Quarterly Journal of Economics*, August 1963, use hourly wage rates multiplied by the average hours in a work year rather than actual annual earnings to calculate net returns. In doing this they avoid the influence of unemployment, and they claim the stronger choice of leisure for the educated. As a practical matter, their method would not yield much different results from the use of actual earnings because the unemployment adjustment would lower their calculated net returns, and the greater, not lesser, work time of the educated would raise them.

[8]William G. Bowen, *Economic Aspects of Education*, Princeton University Press, 1964.

returns upward, insofar as these relatively lower wages reflect a supply response to nonmonetary aspects of prestige, responsibility, etc., associated with these jobs. The greater number attracted to these jobs puts downward pressure on the marginal value product of the particular occupational work force involved so that positive work-related consumption benefits lower the competitive wage.

Bowen realizes that this conclusion depends on a narrow view of social returns, confining them to a strict economic framework. While increased numbers in a field reduce wages in line with the decline in marginal contribution of labor effort to total output, nonmonetary consumption benefits are enjoyed by the workers who have crowded the field. If one takes a broader view of social returns to include consumption benefits, Bowen argues, then the social rate, no less than the private rate, should consider these benefits in estimating net returns.

There is no need to agonize over the question, as far as educational policy is concerned. It depends on the goals and aspirations of the society, reflected in leadership policy. If the national aim is focused on economic growth, then of course the consumption benefits should not be counted. Individual preference for jobs that yield these benefits will push down the returns on them, and they will contribute less to growth at the margin, signaling policy makers to discourage further entry into them.

On the other hand, if public policy is directed to the maximum welfare of the population in the broadest sense of the term to include psychological as well as purely financial returns from public investment, then consumption benefits derived from education should be considered as an addition to financial returns in evaluating social returns to educational investment.

For our society the second approach seems more appropriate. We like to think of ourselves as a nation in which individual welfare, singly or collectively, takes precedence over nationalistic goals, such as military power or economic growth. In fact, there are dangerous aspects of nationalism in a policy that disparaged the social advantage of consumption benefits from education. Public funds would then be directed to programs and students that promised the highest monetary returns. There might be other social goals that would modify the purely economic returns to lead to a broader concept of returns, such as improved race relations and poverty reduction through schooling, but consumption benefits would not be one of them.

We could envision establishment of criteria for the use of public funds for support of schools that stressed vocational or career development in their curriculum and for support of individual students who learned only to earn. Such standards would give little aid to the liberal arts. They would also tend to argue against extensive public financing of education for young women, despite reduction in employment discrimination against them, if the lingering tendency for girls to pursue less vocationally oriented curricula were considered a secondary sex trait.

NONMONETARY RETURNS—EXTERNALITIES

Many favorable by-products outside of direct monetary returns, called "externalities," derive from education which, not captured by the educated individual, redound to the benefit of society as a whole. In fact, they provide public decision makers with an important basis for making educational investments which seem unwise from a straight dollars-and-cents viewpoint and justify public subsidization of education which yield most of their returns to the recipient.

Here we discuss two examples of the externalities, the first, under the heading of general benefits, to include those attributes of education which are acknowledged by all as beneficial to the maintenance of a healthy society and stable government. The second, the contribution of education to economic growth, is less universally held as an unqualified benefit to society.

General Benefits

The private individual may not be concerned with general effects on society of his choice concerning further education. But certainly public authorities must weigh the value of education in such nonquantifiable but crucial areas as the health of the social body, the maintenance of democracy and personal freedom, and the preservation of the social order.

Sometimes the enthusiasm of proponents of education gets out of check, and they claim too much for schooling as a boon to society. Studies show uncertain results in the relationship between school attendance and crime[9] and cast considerable doubt on the effectiveness of compulsory education as a means of reducing the teen-age crime rate. Sociologists find little negative correlation between discrimination and bigotry on the one hand and the level of schooling on the other; education does not mean goodness, and knowledge does not necessarily lead to understanding.

Nevertheless the general social benefits of education, especially in strengthening democratic principles, are considerable. An ignorant people can be misled, if for no other reason than that they are unaware of alternatives. They can be subjugated without educated leaders. It was with much logic, if with complete inhumanity, that during the sorriest period of our history teaching slaves to read and write was made a criminal act. Education strengthens a people's ability to expose the false arguments of the demogogue, to weigh issues, and to choose their leaders wisely, if not always too well. When education reaches the millions and is not just the secret weapon of the few, given man's predilection for freedom, the chances of a society's losing its collective and individual liberty are greatly reduced, despite notable examples to the contrary. The educated mind is trained to inquire and question, not to accept authority by default.

Given that the social goal of preservation of individual freedom is of paramount consideration, how much education must be provided regardless of the weight of all other factors? Few people would question the need of a grade school education to approach this goal. The meager tools of basic literacy do not suffice for understanding the crucial issues of the day, much less allow for rational choice, based on appraisal of the differences between alternative solutions to them.

Because of the tremendous growth and refinement of our modern communications network and the consequent expansion in the volume of information and misinformation available to all, a conservative policy, one which would not wish to gamble on the adequacy of education to permit rational choice among political alternatives in keeping with individual preference, would require the provision of universal education through high school years. If schooling were pressed this far by national policy implemented by provision of sufficient facilities and personnel

[9]O'Donoghue, op. cit., cites British sources that find no reduction in juvenile crime after the school-leaving age was raised.

to service this many students, and by raising the age for compulsory attendance, the concept of education would have to be expanded to include all forms of training in vocational schools and on-the-job, as well as formal, schooling. Otherwise, many not suited to academic training would be channeled into schooling which provided them no benefits in pursuit of greater formal knowledge than they could reasonably acquire. Failure to provide them with additional (vocational) training, while others more proficient at academic work were subsidized through high school, would discriminate in the use of public funds against those with less aptitude for academic work.

In truth, requiring education through age eighteen could be achieved with little change in current policy and practice. Most who can profit economically from this amount of schooling already complete high school. The other able students who do not now receive this much education would probably do so, given greater opportunity and information. Obviously, social goals should include provision of a background favorable for the maximum profitable education for all. By the additional stipulation that all should receive schooling through age eighteen, the state would have to support this requirement by making the extra year or two of advantage to the students who continue schooling because they are forced to, hence the need for expanded vocational and on-the-job training. All this does not assume that our present system requiring schooling to about age seventeen is the best that can be devised by the mind of man. There is no magical formula which says that it is to each student's advantage, and to society's as a whole, that he continue through our current education program until that age. But further discussion of the social value of compulsory education is a theme best treated in the discussion in Chapter 6 of public investment decisions.

By conceding that all should have an education through the high school years, the importance of the general (political) social benefits is acknowledged for the early years of schooling; but at the same time their role in public investment decisions is greatly reduced. Few would argue that college training is essential for providing an electorate capable of maintaining its individual and collective freedom. In short, what is argued here is that the general benefits demand universal high school education or equivalent education, apart from all other considerations, and are of no issue to educational policy makers.

Education and Growth

Every country expresses strong interest in its economic growth rate—
per capita increase in production—and apart from its real contribution
to economic well-being, a high growth rate has replaced the international strength of a country's currency as a national economic prestige
symbol.

In the United States, though, public attitude toward the growth
rate has varied over time. In the post-World War II years, we shared the
general worldwide enthusiasm for a high national growth rate as we saw
strong growth as a way to avoid depression and eliminate poverty. In
addition, a high growth rate was considered points in our favor in the
new national pastime of "keeping up with the Russians," not necessarily
in the narrow military sphere, for only the economically naive would
equate growth per person in a capitalistic economy in which the consumer determined production with military power; more bowling alleys
or beauty parlors per person have little impact on power politics.

In recent years, though, many Americans have become disenchanted
with the total social effect of economic growth. Higher per capital
incomes are in themselves pleasant national occurrences, especially if
they are spread around to all of us. But currently there is concern about
the negative effects of growth on our environment. Even with a stable
population, growth means more production, more waste products, and
more pollution. Ecological extremists are advocating zero economic
growth to accompany zero population increase in their standstill
approach to environmental control. Perhaps there is some validity to
their arguments for the United States, but preachments of the evils of
growth to the poorer countries of the world has all the impact and
credibility of an eighty-year-old haranguing a group of college sopho-
mores against sexual laxity.

Let us assume for the sake of argument that economic growth yields
positive benefits. (A contrary view, with the finding that education
contributed to growth, could lead to the bizarre policy recommendation
that education be curtailed and ignorance exalted, all for the good of
mankind. Perhaps an even worse substitute policy would direct the
thinking of the educated and channel their activities away from ideas,
inventions, and innovations that would contribute to economic growth.)
Confining the definition of growth to an increase in production per

person, rather than in total production, with productive land more or less fixed or limited, growth can come about only through increase in the quantity of capital and improvements in the quality of capital and labor.

Quality improvement in labor can take two forms. First there is the upgrading of the work force. Over the years we have experienced a relative growth in the skilled and professional occupations and decline in the ranks of the unskilled and uneducated. This internal change in the composition of the work force has been accompanied by a second factor contributing to growth, the rise in productivity of workers at all levels of skill. Although it is difficult to measure the quantitative importance of education in these two factors, certainly the added schooling and training our labor has received have provided their share, as they have in other economically advanced countries.

The tie between education and work force upgrading is obvious. Professionals and business executive occupations have grown in size along with the expansion of college and graduate instruction. The trend toward universality in high school completion and the development and widening of vocational training and schooling has led to the expansion of the skilled work force and concomitant decline among the unskilled.

Less obvious is the connection between education and productivity improvement for occupational groups. The simple figures do show higher average educational attainment for workers in every occupational group. At first view this is just to give credit to education for another form of upgrading, this time within specific occupations. But education brings with it knowledge and trains the mind to inquire and to seek new ways of answering old questions, whether they be philosophical or more mundance problems, but more closely related to rising productivity and growth, such as how to build a better mousetrap. In short, growth is aided by the application of education and training to the development of new techniques, production methods, and improvements on machinery, all of which raise the productivity of labor, land, and capital.

While education undoubtedly aids growth, so does the simple expansion of the physical capital stock through investment. Denison has made the most ambitious attempt to measure the contribution of many factors to growth in the United States, including education and physical capital investment.[10] His findings are not conclusive regarding the relative share of each factor, but the issue of relative contribution is important to public policy in countries having a strong goal of economic growth.

The question is of particular importance to developing countries, and the relative merits of human and physical capital investment in speeding and strengthening growth has been rigorously debated. While all agree that education and human capital investment in general have a great deal to offer the growth rate, cogent arguments on the other side emphasize that at least in the early stages of development there might be a greater need for capital equipment to which human capital can be later applied. There is also dispute over whether education should be more academic or vocational.[11] In view of the harshly limited resources of the poorer countries, the controversy is of much more than academic interest.

As far as the United States is concerned, Denison notes that in the area of private decision making higher education has contributed more to economic growth than has capital-goods investment, even though the rate of return on each type of investment was about the same. He makes the point that a great deal of educational investment comes from funds that would otherwise have been used for consumption, while physical capital investments are financed mainly out of money earmarked for savings. Thus, if the educational investment had not been made, there would not have been an equal amount of money transferred to capital-goods production. Denison carefully avoids stating or implying that this differential source for the two types of investment affects their relative rates of return, even if it does explain the greater influence of educational capital on growth.

Elaborating on Denison's point for the future, education undertaken as a result of private investment decisions will also contribute more to economic growth to the extent college expenses are funded out of money that would have otherwise been used for consumption. Of

---

[10]Edward F. Denison, *The Sources of Economic Growth in the United States,* Committee for Economic Development, 1962.

[11]For papers on this controversy, see Mark Blaug (ed.), *Economics of Education I,* Penguin, 1968.

course, this practice has not even an indirect effect on private returns, for it is the rare student indeed who derives much nonmonetary satisfaction from the thought that his schooling will aid his nation's economic growth.

With regard to public investment decisions, the growth rate will have an effect on indirect social returns, and we expect public bodies to take an interest in social benefits derived. But at the same time, whether public money used comes from would-be consumption or savings funds has no influence on the relative contribution of human or physical capital investment to growth. The tax money which the state received undoubtedly would have been partly used for consumption purchases, but the state has the option to use this money for various purposes, only one of which is higher education. Thus the decision regarding public investment to satisfy the policy goal of economic growth must still be based on the relative contribution of each type of investment to growth, the tendency for private educational funds or even tax funds to come substantially out of reduced consumption notwithstanding.

SUMMARY

The effects of the conceptual problems associated with accurate measurement of returns on schooling are rather mixed. In some cases reasonably close estimates can be made or the factors themselves are not very important in decision making, but in others, calculated values can be most reasonably described as rough approximations to reality.

The most serious difficulties arise in measuring direct monetary returns. It is next to impossible to isolate the effect of education from all the other variables that determine earnings; the use of a proxy group to measure foregone after-schooling earnings, and the uncertainty of future returns, add their own sources of error into the calculations.

Modifications to direct returns do little further damage to the precision of estimates. The effect of unemployment should be included, but the conflicting forces of higher unemployment rates and lower earnings for the lesser educated reduce the overall unemployment effect. Furthermore, expanded education might itself lower the average unemployment rate. Mortality and taxes modify returns but are less unpredictable than earnings levels themselves.

Indirect monetary benefits—greater on-the-job training for the educated, option values for intermediate schooling, child-care services provided by schools, etc.—all contribute to returns. But in the main, except for generational transmission of education, they add to the returns of earlier schooling, which are relatively high enough anyway. Social returns from increased work force productivity because of education received by others, admittedly, are difficult to measure.

As for nonmonetary benefits, leisure-related consumption benefits probably have a very small net effect on returns, and work-related benefits which lead to greater work-effort of the educated only support the use of annual earnings as a measure of returns. Consumption benefits from work, though, which result in occupational choice of relatively low-paid jobs are an important source of unquantifiable benefits from education.

Considering externalities, general benefits to society of an educated work force are undeniably great. But they should serve as the basis for providing schooling for all up to age eighteen and have no effect on later investment decision for college. The contribution of education to economic growth may be considerable, but it is difficult to measure; and, further, growth is an example of changing policy goals, which, as discussed in the first chapter, make social investment decisions in education difficult.

CHAPTER FOUR

The Rate
of
Return

Having discussed the costs and returns that enter the rate-of-return approach to investment in education, we turn to the conceptual problems associated with the rate of return itself. The "internal rate of return," derived from these imperfectly measured costs and returns, is simply that rate of discount which equates the present value of returns—earned throughout the future active life of the educated worker—with that of costs—which are mostly incurred shortly after the investment decision is made.

Once this rate is calculated, one more step is required in deciding the economic signal for the investment decision. To conclude whether education "pays" in the crudest economic sense, that is, without regard to the effect of future outside measurable costs and returns, this calculated rate must be compared with the alternative rate of return that would have been earned with the funds that were applied to educational investment. If the calculated internal rate on education exceeds the alternative rate, then apart from indirect and nonmonetary factors that enter the education decision, the rational investor decides on more schooling, with a contrary decision or, more accurately, influence, if the alternative rate is higher.

At issue at this point, then, is the value of this alternative rate, which differs for the borrowing student and the one who finances his schooling, and for private and social investment decisions.

THE PRIVATE ALTERNATIVE RATE OF RETURN

The Borrowing Student

There is nothing mystical about the rate for the borrowing student, which is to be compared with the internal rate of return on his college investment. In the simple extreme case of the student who finances all his schooling costs through loans, the question is not what he would have earned on alternative investments, but, as noted in Chapter 2, the actual interest rate he must pay for his educational loans. The size of loan, or his total schooling cost, does not enter the analysis, nor at this stage should we worry about the current shortage of loan funds for education.

The market rate that must be paid, even in the absence of true market imperfections that limit the availability of this type of credit, is very high because of the illiquid and risky nature of the loans. "Very high" can be translated to mean higher than the going rate of return (profit) on business investment, which is much more liquid and less risky.

Unlike the holder of physical capital, the individual cannot divest himself of his human capital; he cannot transfer his investment in himself, once made, into other investments, nor even sell it for scrap value. There are some exceptions. For example, the lawyer who would switch to pharmacy would find his general education of some value as a basis for grafting on a new professional skill to his existing knowledge. He might even gain the best of both worlds by later serving in the legal department of a pharmaceutical firm. An economics professor who switches to farming can write a textbook first, allowing for returns on an investment he will no longer operate.

The imagination can conjure up other special cases in which human investments can be made to resemble those in plant and machinery. But certainly, for the most part, the former are more like sunk costs.

Add the risk related to the uncertainty of the quality of the product resulting from human investment. When a firm buys new machinery and equipment, the purchasing department makes a careful selection of the item best suited to the firm's needs. How efficiently the firm employs the capital acquired is another matter, but is has little uncertainty about the machine's capabilities and surely none about its willingness to perform up to its potential.

The student, on the other hand, has no assurance about the quality of his investment. A contributor to this uncertainty is the length of time it takes, four years for a college degree, to form the investment. In fact, the student is not even sure that he will complete the investment project. In the intermediate stages, either the college or the student himself might decide to discontinue further investment in his education. The rates on partial investment in a degree program are very low, a phenomenon to be discussed in the next two chapters. Relevant to the issue here, this low rate means that the possibility of not finishing a course of study adds to the special risks of educational investment.

The above described elements of illiquidity and special risks apply to the student who finances his own schooling as well as to the borrowing student who has them reflected in the higher rate he would have to pay the lender. If these were the only factors that made college investment risky to the lender, then except for true capital market imperfections of credit limitation that made loan rates above competitive equilibrium, the borrowing student would pay the same interest rate as the foregone rate of the affluent student who financed his own schooling. The difference in financing would have no effect on the comparative "alternative" rate with which the internal rate of return would be compared.

But the borrowing student has to pay more on the capital market than the self-financing student could earn from a different investment with the same illiquidity and risks already discussed. In the absence of government subsidization or repayment guarantee, possibilities which lie outside of the framework of the present discussion, the lending agency would demand higher rates because of the nature of the loan itself. For one thing, the loan is not clearly self-liquidating. Returns may be earned from the investment to allow for repayment, but the tie between loan and earnings on it are not as close as on business loans. More serious are the problems associated with collection. If "poor management" of human capital leads to low returns and ability to service the loan, the lending bank can do nothing about it. No tangible assets are produced in the investment process, and banks cannot reclaim individuals. This is to say nothing about the mobility of human capital and the difficulty of tracking down reluctant repayers. Lending officers may be impressed by solemn promises to repay out of future earnings, but these assurances do not have the simple attraction of a mortgage on a house or factory.

While the self-financing student also faces the risk of an illiquid investment, he does not face the possibility of defaulting on a loan because of it, nor does he need bother about collection costs on a mobile asset, risk factors for which the lending institution must be compensated.

The Self-financing Student

Because of capital market imperfection, the alternative of making loans as inherently risky as those to finance college education may not be readily available to individuals. Thus there is some question as to the correct value of the alternative rate, or the opportunity cost of the rate of return on college investment.

The student could have invested in physical capital with money used to pay for school costs, whether in portfolio investments of corporations or, more similar to educational investment, in a single proprietorship, and earned an average rate of 8 to 10 percent. Does not the educated, human capitalist require enterpreneurial skills as he applies his capital to work that leads him to the highest monetary and psychic returns?

This physical capital can serve as his opportunity cost for his school investment, but this is not the same thing as saying that if the internal rate of return on educational investment is at least as high as that on physical capital, opportunity costs will be covered, and the economic conditions for choice for schooling will have been met. The opportunity cost refers to the rate on a less risky investment; therefore the threshhold internal rate for a decision in favor of school investment must be higher by an amount equal to the value of the extra risk factor. Analogously, the wage on an unpleasant job that meets the opportunity-cost wage on a pleasant one is higher than the foregone wage.

Note that the concept of opportunity cost loses none of its power if an activity similar to the one practiced cannot be undertaken. If capital market imperfections prevent alternative loans similar to those in education, then the measurement of opportunity cost becomes more difficult since there is no handy actual rate for comparison. But conceptually, opportunity cost simply becomes the rate on a distantly related type of investment, in this case physical capital, with an upward adjustment for risk that would make the investor indifferent to a choice between a schooling investment at the higher adjusted rate and the actual physical capital rate. It is the uncertainty over the *size* of the adjustment that makes it more difficult to assign a value to opportunity costs when there are no parallel alternative investments.

In any case, the "alternative rate" for the borrowing student, the rate he must pay on his loan, against which the internal rate of return is compared, is higher than the opportunity-cost alternative rate for the self-financing student. Thus, economic motivation for investment in education is weaker for the poorer student who must borrow to pay for his schooling.

Alternative Rates for Specific Occupations

Higher interest rates for human capital borrowing, and for consumption purposes as well, than for business loans are less a reflection of imperfection in the capital market than of the risk of unsecured loans. These differential rates should be taken into account in comparing the net returns to investment in education for specific occupations.

Undoubtedly, the higher internal rate of return on an investment in a medical education than in engineering is largely caused by monopoly elements in medicine. Limitations of medical training facilities, not responsive to market forces, prevent an expanded supply of doctors from driving the rate down to competitive levels.

But consideration of relevant interest rates narrows the monopolistic gains to doctors, which the simple internal rate-of-returns comparison registers. Medical training is long and expensive. Even with an expansion of potential supply of medical students, many would be deterred by the high cost of student loans, which make financing of medical schooling expensive, more so than for engineering with its lower costs and consequent lesser pressure to borrow. In short, the appropriate rate for comparison with the internal rate of return would be high for the borrowing medical student.

But the same high cost of borrowing on the shaky collateral of expected future earnings may also partially explain the higher internal rate for medicine on grounds related to the timing of earnings streams. Engineers earn more in the early postschooling years and enjoy their peak incomes long before doctors, who obtain a higher internal rate because of their very large earnings in later years of their work life. Thus, total lifetime earnings differences between the two occupations far exceed the differences in the present value of their earnings at age eighteen.

Time preferences for money vary during an individual's lifetime. In the early years, with thin resources, low income but good prospects, and high consumption needs and wants, the typical medical student and recent graduate have strong preferences for current over future dollars. With market interest rates below subjective rates, they are likely to borrow, both for consumption purposes and for financing education. The young engineer may earn enough to cover his consumption needs, but the young doctor will often have to borrow to supplement his low earnings. Of course the individual doctor may have outside resources to cover his budget, even including a working wife, but we are discussing the effect of a widening income stream on the whole population of doctors. Some will borrow at the high rates for consumption loans that are backed only by future earning power.

To the extent of this borrowing, adjustment must be made in estimating the economic returns to investment in medical education because of the higher rate paid for education and consumption loans. The alternative, opportunity-cost rate for comparison with the internal rate must be a higher composite rate for doctors that includes the high rate for schooling and consumption loans, the weight of these factors determined by the difference in proportion of school costs covered by loans between the two professions, and the number of years the average doctor borrows.

While the size of the adjustment is uncertain, it makes sense to claim that the variations in the time pattern of their income streams lead to overstatement of the financial advantage to a career in medicine over one in engineering by unqualified comparison of internal rates of return alone. The higher alternative rate, or opportunity interest cost, for medicine closes part of the gap in net returns created by the monopoly elements in the market for doctors.

THE SOCIAL ALTERNATIVE RATE OF RETURN

Just as in the case of the direction of economic factors in private educational investment decisions, to find the economic influence through the rate-of-return approach on public, or social, investment decisions requires comparison of an alternative, foregone, opportunity-cost rate with the calculated internal social rate of return. Before going into the particular problems that arise in establishing the alternative rate for social investment, this is a good place to reexamine the differences between the private and social internal rate itself.

The Private and Social Internal Rate Compared

The social rate is not confined to considerations of public decision making. It does not represent the economist's contribution to etatism at its worst, with public authorities waiting for a faint signal from uncertain dollars-and-cents cost-benefit calculations to make binding educational investment decisions, all in the national interest. Rather, the social rate referesto something broader and more indefinite than the role of government in education. As its name implies, its frame of reference is society as a whole, but it can be applied to any social body, no matter how small.

As such, there is no contradiction in terms to speak of the social rate of return on private universities. From a financial rather than an administrative aspect, it is becoming increasingly difficult these days to distinguish between private and public universities. The former could not survive without substantial direct and indirect government aid, and the latter maintain a healthy interest in individual and foundation contributions. Be that as it may, even if private universities received no public funds, a social rate would exist different from the private rate, which considers only the costs incurred by the individual students and the returns that accrued to them.

If, as is certainly not the case, all direct costs were financed by tuition, the private and social rates would be equal.[1] But social and private returns would differ. Considering only direct monetary returns, private returns include only the extra spendable income received as a result of education; social returns take a more global interest and include the gains not only to the educated but also to the rest of society, with total gains measured by the taxable income difference resulting from education, under the heroic assumption that the government spends its tax money for the benefits of us all.

While the returns are higher for the social rate, the costs are too, to the extent actual payment by students falls short of full-cost tuition. Studies, at least for the United States,[2] show no clear-cut difference for the two rates, with higher social returns just about canceling out higher costs.

[1]We again exclude nonpublic foundation or individual contribuitons to students in grants and scholarships from *private* financing, which refers to funds of the student and his family and not to nongovernment, as opposed to public, funding.

[2]Mark Blaug, "The Private and the Social Returns on Investment in Education: Some Results for Great Britain," *Journal of Human Resources,* Summer 1967, finds higher private than social rates for Great Britain, where so much of college funding is by the state.

Trying to find which internal rate is larger in a given instance has no policy meaning since they are not competitive inasmuch as the private rate refers to individual decisions and the social rate to public ones. Nevertheless, study of the different components that enter into the calculation of the two rates helps clarify understanding of their interpretation.

Perhaps, since the social rate treats all costs and returns and since the word "social" may possibly connote concentration on the government sector, the expression "total rate" would more appropriately describe the internal rate at issue.[3] While this term has not gained wide currency, we must keep in mind that the social rate has both a broader and simpler meaning than as a guide for national welfare decisions. It signals whether the revenues devoted to a human capital project, in this case education, have been economically wisely invested, that is, whether the rate that discounts all monetary returns to total investment costs exceed those on alternative investments.

All this does not deny that for practical purposes the social internal rate will apply closely to state educational investment decisions. Government at any level will find the rate useful if it wishes to have economic factors help serve in establishing priorities among alternative public investment projects. For social policy, there is little control over the effect of private decisions on social economic welfare, and interest is in the economic value of public schooling investment decisions, measured by the social rate of return.

As with the private rate, the social rate faces the unfair charge that it will be used to lift economic factors above all others in the choice of investment projects from limited public funds. The refutation is also the same; all factors should be counted, and economic ones should not be ignored. Apart from differences in measurement, the special feature, noted in Chapter 2, that plagues attempts at accurate measurement of social rates relates to the flexibility in law and custom that society can adopt and that allows for differences in rates under different sociolegal frameworks. In addition, to be expanded upon in Chapter 6, the true social rate must consider whether the measured social gains from education are not at least in part spurious in that they are simply returns to those who receive schooling with no gain in total output because of the education in question.

---

[3] W. Lee Hansen, "Total and Private Rates of Return to Investment in Schooling," *Journal of Political Economy*, vol. 71, April 1963, introduces the concept of the "total rate."

The Alternative Social Rate

For social, just as much as for private, educational investment, an alternative rate on foregone investments plays a crucial role in the determination of whether or not education "pays" in the narrow direct rate-of-return sense. But public support of education operates under different financial constraints and alternatives than priavte financing.

Capital market imperfections that limit borrowing are fewer for all levels of government. Individual risks and the peculiar illiquidity of human capital investment to the lenders are minimized by larger-scale investments. More importantly, government borrowing for almost any purpose, even backed only by the promise of repayment out of general funds, can be secured more easily and cheaply than by the lone private investor. The government has a better credit rating.

Consequently, the opportunity-cost rate for government financed education lies below the rate for private investment. In fact, the government could lower the private rate and encourage further private investment by guaranteeing loans, thereby substituting its borrowing power for the individual's. Of course, the government would then merely be assuming the peculiar risks of individual investors in education away from the reluctant banks and would in effect be subsidizing private borrowers. This potential loss to the government, measured by the difference between the guaranteed rate and the free-market rate for student loans, could be considered as the government's payment to individuals for socially beneficial externalities arising from education. But we are now entering a field of educational policy reserved for discussion in the last chapter.

In an unrestricted world, with the government borrowing as much as it wanted within the single constraint of economic efficiency, the correct value for the opportunity rate to government would be either its borrowing cost (rate) for long-term loans or its equal rate, on alternative government projects. In the real world of limited borrowing power, the latter rate, which included an assigned money value for all social benefits and externalities, would be the correct measure of the alternative rate.

Considering only direct economic costs and returns, social benefits are maximized when rates of return are equalized on all investment projects.

If the rate of return on a highway exceeds that on a college, then the investment should be made in it and not in the college. The question arises over the current economic decision if the rate of return on both investments exceeds the rate the state must pay on borrowed funds. Contrary to first impressions, it does not follow that both investments should be undertaken. If loan funds are limited, the state should invest in the highway, which yields the higher return.

Only when the marginal rates are equalized, after further highway construction reduces the marginal rate to that of the college, should equal future investment be made in both, assuming, of course, that the equalized rate exceeds that on borrowed funds, a situation that exists under conditions of capital market imperfection.[4]

In any case, though, the raw money rate, unadjusted for social non-monetary benefits, would be lower than the alternative rate for private investors because of the absence of the special risks on government educational loans. We assume no special advantages of nonmonetary benefits to society over those falling to the individual. Furthermore, as has been mysteriously hinted, there are some indications that calculation of the social internal rate for recent investment in education tends to overstate the true rate. As for the actual alternative rates, they can only be educated guesses, and, given today's interest rate structure, we have no reason to consider as unrealistic rates of at least 10 percent for the private opportunity-cost rate and at most that rate for government-financed social investment in education.

RATE-OF-RETURN FINDINGS

Calculations of the rate of return for various levels of schooling have been made with great care and the pursuit of accuracy, within the limitations of the conceptual shortcomings of any result derived. Studies show a declining trend in rates of return with level of education, from grade school through graduate school. Individual studies show variations in the rates of return because of differences in estimating techniques in methods of isolating the influence of education on earnings, in groups and time periods covered. Table 4-1 summarizes calculated rates of return from a few well-known studies.[5]

---

[4]Lester Thurow, *Investment in Human Capital,* Wadsworth, 1970, offers a tight analysis of the interest rate–alternative rate relationship in his intensive theoretical study of human capital.

[5]Elchanan Cohn, *The Economics of Education,* Heath, 1972, chap. 7, presents an exhaustive review of numerous studies.

TABLE 4-1

Rates of return on investment in schooling

Level of schooling	Study, %				
	Schultz	Becker	Hansen	Hanoch	Ashenfelter-Mooney
Grade school	35(1949)		15.0(1949)		
High school	14(1939)	16(1939)	14.5(1949)		
		20(1949)		16.1(1959)	
		25(1956)			
		28(1958)			
College		14.5(1939)	10.1(1949)	9.6(1959)	
		13.0(1949)			
		12.4(1956)			
		14.8(1958)			
Graduate					
(1 yr +)					
(M.A.)					7.8(1960)
(Ph.D.)					
3 yr					10.8(1960)
4 yr					9.1(1960)
5 yr					7.1(1960)

Sources: Theodore W. Schultz, "Education and Economic Growth," in H. S. Rickey (ed.), *Social Forces Influencing American Education,* Chicago, 1961, chap. 3.

Gary S. Becker, *Human Capital,* National Bureau of Economic Research, 1964, chaps. 4 and 6.

W. Lee Hansen, "Total and Private Rates of Return to Investment in Schooling," *Journal of Political Economy,* vol. 71, April 1963.

Giora Hanoch, "An Economic Analysis of Earnings and Schooling," *Journal of Human Resources,* vol. 2, Summer 1967.

Orley Ashenfelter and Joseph D. Mooney, "Some Evidence on the Private Returns to Graduate Education," *Southern Economic Journal,* vol. 35, January 1969.

The grade school rates are social rates, with private rates considered infinite. All other figures are for private rates. Hansen derives values of 11.4 percent and 10.2 percent for social rates for high school and college, respectively.

Unfortunately, the studies are not very current, especially the ones on earlier schooling. But the high rates on grade school and high school investment suggest that they are well above the level of marginal decision making. Even if the argument advanced earlier that the social benefits from early schooling justified investment to assure completion of high school, or its equivalent in years of vocational training, no matter what the monetary returns, were not universally supported, the returns themselves support the need for universal education at this level. Some investment decisions for early schooling do remain, despite the high rate, and these will be discussed in Chapter 6.

As we approach the level of a high school education for all, most of our concern narrows on the wisdom of investing further, in college and beyond. If we accept a rate of 10 percent for the upper limit private opportunity-cost rate and lower limit for the social, then there does not seem to be any clear-cut evidence of underinvestment in higher education. If we struck an average for the three studies on college returns and assumed that this were the current rate, we would arrive at an 11 percent level,[6] a little higher than the suggested alternative private rate of 10 percent.

But the college rates in Table 4-1 for Becker and Hanoch are for white urban and white Northern males, respectively, the highest earning work force groups. For 1939, Becker calculated a rate of about 10 percent for nonwhites, and Hanoch for 1959 a rate of only 6 percent for Southern nonwhites. These results show that much lower returns from college for nonwhites outweighed their lower direct and mainly indirect—forgone earnings—costs.

Thus, taking all the data into consideration, it is not unrealistic to state that overall the average private rate of return on investment in college is about the same as that on alternative investments, using an opportunity-cost rate of 10 percent to include the special risk factors associated with investment in schooling. At least we will argue from that position in the following policy chapter.

We only have Hansen's study for the social rate of return on college, and his finding is an almost identical rate close to 10 percent for the two. This means that the higher social costs, representing the deviation

---

[6]Hanoch's rate should probably be given the most weight because he included the most variables in his calculation of returns from education alone.

from full-cost tuition, are about offset by increased tax revenues from the college educated. This internal rate is somewhat higher than our working guess of a 10 percent maximum for the opportunity-cost rate for public investments. But recall, we promise to explain that there is a tendency for the calculated internal rate to overstate the true social economic gain from college education. Again, we can claim with some degree of realism that the data, at least the calculations from one study, do not indicate significant public underinvestment in college.

The graduate figures are interesting. Further education, without definite attainment of an advanced degree, yields low returns (Hanoch). Ashenfelter and Mooney find a low rate of only 7.8 percent for a two-year M.A. They find a rate for the doctorate, earned in three years, about the same as the rate for college and also for the assumed alternative rate. Most doctorates take longer to complete their program, and the rate trails off into a losing investment, with the 10 percent estimate for the alternative rate. What is more, their study is of Woodrow Wilson fellows, an educational elite, who may be expected to profit more than the average from advanced schooling.[7]

Furthermore, with many graduate students subsidized by scholarship aid and with much of the funds coming from public sources, the social rate would probably be significantly lower for each of the three time periods in attaining the degree. This study suggests public overinvestment in graduate education.

Ashenfelter and Mooney find that the rate of return differs depending on the area in which the degree is earned, with the highest returns for those who specialize in the sciences and lowest for those who get their degrees in the humanities. We look further into these findings in the next chapter, but a simple explanation suggests itself. Perhaps the humanists derive greater consumption benefits during their work life. Perhaps.

[7]These are much higher rates than the 1 to 3 percent range for the Ph.D. found in an earlier 1947 study, Shane Hunt, "Income Determinants for College Graduates and the Return to Educational Investment," *Yale Economic Essays*, Fall 1963. Lynn Maxwell, "Some Evidence on Negative Returns to Graduate Education," *Western Economic Journal*, vol. 7, June 1970, finds a high 12.6 percent for a four-year doctorate for 1965 University of Nebraska graduates, but his group includes professionals such as dentists as well as Ph.D. holders.

THE MANPOWER-FORECASTING APPROACH
TO EDUCATIONAL INVESTMENT DECISIONS

The weakness of the rate-of-return approach, with its conceptual problems that prevent accurate measurement of the relevant variables, has encouraged support for other guides to educational planning. The most popular of these alternatives is the manpower-forecasting approach.[8] In its simplest form it signals (higher) educational investment—and we abstract from vocational training—in those fields for which forecasted labor market demand is strongest.

Having stated that the rate-of-return approach offers the best guide to the economic influence on educational planning even after detailing many of its shortcomings, with more to follow, and preparing to discuss policy decisions based on this approach, these pages have a vested interest in arguing the superiority of the method over the manpower-forecasting approach. Hopefully, though, the following argument in its support is based more on objective reasoning than on self-interest.

That the forecasting approach is obviously and admittedly vocationally oriented is not its greatest failing. Consumption benefits and secondary externalities are ignored in the internal analysis, but so are they too in the rate-of-return approach. In public decisions on education, they could be considered in directing investment into fields which promised more of these "spillovers," even if the actual forecasted demand were not strong. But against the approach, it should be acknowledged that this is less likely to happen when planning is made on a narrow, almost occupational, basis than on the total view of schooling of the rate-of-return method. As for private decisions, the individual can consider his tastes and interests along with forecasted demand in pursuing a career goal.

A main criticism of forecasting relates to the difficulty in predicting specific occupational demand in a world of changing relative prices and wages. Predicted shortages can be removed by factor substitution and a change in relative wages that reduces the demand for the scarce labor. Again, we really do not have too serious a shortcoming here. Added

---

[8]Richard S. Eckaus, "Economic Criteria for Education and Training," *Review of Economics and Statistics,* vol. 46, May 1964, presents a detailed application of the manpower-forecasting approach to educational planning.

supply of the demanded labor might forestall or temper the wage adjustments. Factor substitutability works both ways. Predicted shortages would be reflected in higher expected returns in the rate-of-return approach and would signal investment in these areas.

A seeming advantage of forecasting is that it directs attention to specific needs, while rate-of-return analysis, except for a few studies, centers on education as a whole. This is perhaps a fault of data shortage or simply lack of research in the rate-of-return approach. There is no conceptual reason why rates cannot be calculated for specific fields, but if this were done, the rate-of-return approach would run the same danger of emphasizing vocational aspects of education in government planning that characterizes the manpower-forecasting method.

We shall discuss later a glaring weakness of the rate-of-return approach in that it treats earnings as an unqualified measure of economic contribution to society. In avoiding this source of error, though by not dealing with money returns (earnings), the manpower-forecasting method loses all capacity to guide investment decisions toward achieving economic efficiency.

The manpower-forecasting method has been criticized for not considering costs in its decision-making apparatus. But this is a logical omission. Costs would only be useful as an economic factor in relation to returns, and since the method eschews returns, the dollar value of costs would dangle with no comparable value to which they can apply themselves. There is the pounds and yards problem here in deciding whether program A is more beneficial than B if it costs 20 percent more in dollars and enjoys a 20 percent higher expected demand in trained workers. Ideally, the manpower approach can tell you whether there will be a strong demand for lawyers. But only cost-benefit analysis can suggest whether a career in law would be more profitable than in some other field of study or whether the greatest returns would be missed by investing in any area of education instead of business.

The rate-of-return method provides the (imperfect) means of deciding the efficiency of investment in human capital (education) compared to physical capital, based on comparison of internal rates of return and alternative opportunity-cost rates, and its analysis could be applied to economic efficiency in maximization of net returns—for particular fields of study, The manpower-forecasting approach does not even address these problems.

SUMMARY

A main theme of this chapter is the search for the alternative rate of interest against which the internal rate of return on educational investment can be compared to determine the allocative efficiency in using private and public funds. For the borrowing student, the rate is simply the loan cost on student loans, a rate much higher than for business loans because of the peculiar risks of investment in human capital.

If the capital market operated perfectly, the individual with adequate resources could direct these funds to the financing of someone else's education instead of his own. But even if he could do so, the opportunity cost of self-financing would be lower than the rate the student borrower pays because the risks of loan default and collection costs do not relate to self-financing.

Risk-pooling and a stronger credit position, and limited alternative investments, lower the opportunity-cost rate for public financing of loans. While the social rate applies to the question of *total* efficiency of educational investment, policy issues center on *public* investment for the social rate and individual choice for the private rate.

The data do not suggest pronounced private or social underinvestment in higher education. For college, the private alternative rate is not significantly above the roughly estimated opportunity-cost rate of 10 percent for other (physical capital) investments. For graduate education, especially for schooling that does not lead to a degree, and for drawn out degree programs, there is indeed evidence of overinvestment in a narrow economic sense.

According to the limited evidence, this social rate for college is about the same as the private rate. But despite the lower alternative rate for public human capital investments, there is support for the view of overall optimum social investment in college, because, as will be discussed in Chapter 6, there is more than a hint that actual earnings are something greater than the true monetary contribution to total production of the work efforts of the educated.

Despite the weaknesses in the rate-of-return approach it offers the best means for making education policy decisions based on economic factors. At best, the manpower-forecasting approach can only point out fields of greatest future need (demand) but cannot help answer the questions we will be asking in the next two chapters. Are there economic grounds for a given individual to go to college? To go to graduate school? To drop out of school? To prepare for a particular career? Has society invested too much in college? In graduate education? How can we best maximize the economic efficiency of educational investment dollars? To begin to answer these questions we require some form of cost-benefit analysis which the rate-of-return method provides.

CHAPTER FIVE

The Individual Investment Decision

Rate-of-return data can serve as a helpful but imperfect guide to private educational investment decisions. Individuals include economic considerations by varying degrees in their occupational choice, even when they are somewhat obscured by nonmonetary elements.

Guidance counselors use manpower forecasts to channel youthful ambition toward practical goals. We need not refer to the classic cases of the glass blower or the blacksmith to emphasize that career preference must adjust to labor market realities.

But while manpower forecasts provide some economic information for educational investment decisions, internal rate-of-return estimates allow for more pointed measurement of the relative economic benefits among various educational investments. In fact, the estimates aid in making the basic decision whether to make any additional investment at all.

This chapter examines the individual educational investment decision in the light of all its components discussed previously. Then we turn to the timing of the decision and the question of whether or not to continue with a program—the dropout issue. Finally, we focus again on the role of consumption benefits in investment and occupational choice. Throughout, the individual is assumed to be maximizing his welfare, or utility, or however we wish to designate the mix of economic and nonmonetary features of educational investment. In short, he follows a literal meaning of policy: "management of (his) affairs based on (his) material interest." Thus for the individual the policy issue is not what goal to follow, but what choices to make to maximize his welfare.

FACTORS IN THE DECISION

Rate-of-return data provide the prospective private investor with very indefinite economic information. To see the practical limitation of these calculations, consider as an example an eighteen-year-old who is weighing a decision of a career in sales. He has an interest in selling and is ready to go ahead with a lengthy expensive educational investment, provided the economic prospects look promising. Assume we provide him with favorable rate-of-return data, that is a rate high enough that allows his interest to outweigh higher potential rates in other fields which have less appeal to him, and higher than the rate on physical capital, modified upwards by the special risks in educational investment. Assume further that data are in refined form, corrected as carefully as possible for expected unemployment, taxes, and mortality.

But the young man realizes that statistics do not apply to the individual. He knows that the average rate is calculated from a wide range of particular rates, some of them very low indeed, which reflect vast differences in annual and lifetime earnings among individual salesmen. Earnings vary because of the range in quality of the investment itself, in the entrepreneurial skill of the investor in finding and holding good jobs, in labor effort applied to the embodied investment, in helpful personal contacts, and in just plain luck. At the vantage point of eighteen years of age, from which his time horizon extends, the youth does not know how these factors will influence his future earnings. He does not even know what he will be selling; it may be steel products, textbooks, drugs, or office machinery. Each might benefit from some specialized education, but he might decide a general academic curriculum with a sprinkling of business courses will allow a maximum flexibility within an appropriate framework for a sales career.

As an added problem, rate-of-return data refer to past experience, but the eighteen-year-old is interested in future prospects. Estimation of earnings twenty and thirty years hence requires more imagination than knowledge.

If the eighteen-year-old is a black or a woman, the handicap of actual discrimination cannot be ignored. The larger correction for unemployment and smaller expected earnings differences attributable to education would lead to a lower internal rate of return than for the young white male. Even if rates of return are available for those with characteristics subject to earnings and employment discrimination, the individual investment decision would be influenced by uncertainty regarding future attitudes and practices.

On the favorable side, the prospective investor knows that employment and earnings preference are currently given to college graduates. He does not know, though, how much the reported earnings differences between college and high school graduate salesmen is attributable to the greater skill and productivity resulting from college time and how much to employer preference for college graduates. From a monetary point of view, he does not much care, except that he has no way of knowing whether he will enjoy the same, more, or less preference as present college graduate salesmen.

Timing of the Investment Decision

Given all these uncertainties, it might seem that the young man's safest course would be to defer his investment decision. Except that the passage of time permits new experiences and the development of interests, so that his attitudes toward a selling career may become more definite, time works against the economic profitability of investment in education—assuming information about the future gets no clearer just from pushing the time horizon forward.

Since we do not live forever, what might have been a profitable human investment at eighteen may no longer be so at thirty-five. Foregone earnings rise with age and experience, and when investment is undertaken in the middle years, the remaining period of work life is probably too short for the higher earnings resulting from education to make the high-cost investment profitable.

Even if we retained our vigor and lived forever, it would still prove more profitable to undertake educational investments at an early age. With endless life, decisions on later investment may become positive because the period of net returns from education would extend indefinitely. There would be more economically rational career switching and development made at age fifty-six, or for that matter, at three hundred fifty-six.

But the issue here is not whether investment pays at any age but whether it is more profitable to undertake a given investment at a younger age. Perhaps an interpersonal comparison will clarify the economic gains to early investment. Assume that with an everlasting work life, at any age investing in preparation for a career in sales pays; that is, the present value of future returns exceeds that of costs, or the internal rate of return exceeds the adjusted rate on alternative physical capital investments. A begins his college education at eighteen, while B, who is similar in every respect related to earnings, works at a high school graduate job for twelve years and begins his college investment at thirty. Meanwhile, B has been investing his future college costs at the lower upward adjusted rate earned on corporate equities.

The internal rates of return must be calculated from the total investment decisions. For A the rate is simple enough, being at the level which equates the discounted eternal lifetime returns to current education costs. For B, though, the rate becomes a composite of the modified rate on alternative investments for the first twelve-years—in fact the rate is earned from alternative investments—and the larger rate from the investment transferred to education at age thirty. This internal rate, of course, still exceeds that from continued investment in physical capital, but, what matters here, falls short of that for A who began his career development at age eighteen.

Expressed more simply, perhaps with reference to the future instead of the present, after age forty-five or so, when investment costs for both are completed and each has gone through the low earnings years at the start of his career, A and B will have identical annual earnings from work—unto eternity. But A will always have the extra income from his earlier start in educational investment. If both consumed within their means, this extra income would have been invested, yielding A higher annual income than B forever. Though they lived and worked forever, B would find A's living standard as unattainable as the maiden to the youth on the Grecian Urn, and for the same reason—they never change their relative positions.

Thus, for the eighteen-year-old, now is the best time to make his decision whether to invest in the education required for a sales career. He wants to make a rational, utility-maximizing choice. He knows his subjective nonmonetary preference, but even this may change with time. He burdens his judgment with all the uncertainties and imponderables that make the estimated rate of return for *his own* investment a crude guide to the weight monetary considerations should carry in his decision. The only sound advice the economic data can give him is that if his estimated internal rate of return is not relatively extremely low, he should follow his star. But this advice is of small value to the youth who planned to do just that anyway.

DROPPING OUT OF SCHOOL

The rate of return on completing any school program—high school, college, or graduate school—is significantly higher than the rate on partial completion; the dropout fares much worse than the graduate.[1] On the surface, then, dropping out seems an unwise (uneconomic) move.

In fact, public sentiment is against premature school leaving, and the term "dropout" carries a connotation of some form of academic waste product. Exhortations on matchbook covers and government sponsored television spot commercials advising against dropping out, oddly enough, are usually based on an economic appeal. In truth, if the potential dropout used the average rates of return on full schooling compared to the dropout rate as his guide, economic forces would influence him to finish school.

But he knows that statistics do not apply to the individual, and average rates of return on school completion do not relate to him anyway. The average dropout is not the average student. His grades are worse, his interest in school weaker, his chance for profitable investment in further schooling, measured by any customary criteria, less. They offer bad and deceptive advice, who use the bait of average rates on school completion to attract the would-be dropout to further costly investment in schooling in search of returns he cannot capture.

All this does not deny that many who plan to quit before finishing would profit from staying in school. Just because a student makes a decision to leave school does not mean he has made a wise one. But

[1] For example, Gary Becker, *Human Capital*, National Bureau of Economic Research, 1964, p. 93, found internal rates of return for dropouts some four points below the rate for college graduates and far enough below 10 percent to suggest "some college" is a relatively unprofitable investment.

this is an individual matter and staying in school should not be recommended for all.

The student who makes an economically sound decision of dropping out will most likely realize a smaller return on his educational investment than the average student who finishes the program, but not less than *he* would net were he to go on to try to finish. On average, though, he will find that this schooling level was a bad investment for him, one that yielded a lower rate than the adjusted rate on alternative physical capital investment. At the time he began, say, his college investment at age eighteen, he thought it was going to be a profitable one, but he is not the first or last to make bad investments. Few beginning students plan to cut short their schooling; no more than anyone else is the dropout given the gift of prescience.

As the educational level rises, costs per student-year increase, both for direct tuition and fees and indirect foregone earnings. At the same time, the net returns from successful completion of the degree program, compared with early leaving, are well above the levels for early schooling. This puts a great deal of economic pressure on the student weighing quitting college against continuing his studies. Taking an individual rather than social view of the situation, he does not care that his extra earnings from degree attainment might result not so much from greater knowledge acquired during the last years of education as from employer and general labor market preference for holders of degree certificates. If he can appraise his own chances realistically, he can admit that his gains from education will be less than average and might even make his total investment in the schooling program an economically unwise one in that he would have gained more from an alternative use of his time and money. But his vantage point, the time from which his time horizon extends, is not at the beginning of the program but somewhere through it. He knows that he has already invested a great deal of money and that the net returns for "some college" or "some graduate training" over the next earlier completed schooling level are very low.

The economic issue of whether to continue, though, has nothing to do with this past experience. The only factor that counts is whether the rate of return on investing in the remaining years to completion is above the alternative rate, which it is likely to be for college, and especially for graduate school, even for the weaker student. It is not a question of throwing good money after bad; the investment decision is always a marginal one and not conditioned by past experience.

To explain this numerically, if a college student has completed two years of a four-year program and expects a rate of return of 6 percent on this two years of post-high school education, economic influences signal him to quit, assuming a 10 percent threshhold value for positive choice, if he figures that his rate on the next two years' investment will be only 9 percent even though the average graduate nets 15 percent on his last two years. The higher the average marginal rate on the final two years, the less likely any individual student will appraise his chances as poorly as to decide to drop out, and thus the lower the dropout rate.

The result is interesting if his expected marginal rate is, say, 11 percent, a rate above the assumed threshhold for positive decision but low enough to make his total college investment a losing one. This is not good money going after bad but making the most out of a bad initial decision. He would have gained more—and, to emphasize, we are only isolating monetary influences in this analysis—by not having gone to college at all. But after two years of sunk costs, he does better to go on even if he does not turn an unsuccessful total investment into a profitable one because he can gain more from a further investment in schooling than on other investments if he quits. He has reached the point, to misquote the Bard slightly, "when it would be more tedious to turn back than to go o'er."

A propos of this discussion of the marginal nature of the dropout decision, Ashenfelter and Mooney offer two explanations why graduate students took five years to earn their Ph.D.'s when the rate of return (7.1 percent) is so much lower than for those who finished in three years. They claim that some took longer in order to avoid military service and because they enjoyed being graduate students, deriving consumption benefits while being educated. Given existing draft rules at the time, we will not cavil at the first explanation, and will also admit some, but not much, validity to the second because it assumes that those who stay longer derive more fun out of graduate schooling than those who finish earlier.

But this reasoning assumes that there is something called a three-year Ph.D. program and another called a five-year program. In reality the completion time is open-ended. Related to the previous discussion, a different explanation for the choice for a longer graduate period suggests itself. Even among these superior students in the Ashenfelter-Mooney group, there were some having difficulty with their graduate work. At the outset they did not *choose* a five-year program, with its low return.

But having spent time and money in further study in the first years after their B.A. degree, they decided that it would be more profitable to press on to completion, even if, by taking longer, the overall internal rate for the stretched-out Ph.D. was below that on alternative investments. The implication of this explanation is that the *marginal* rate of return on the last years of schooling was high—higher than on alternative investments.

CONSUMPTION BENEFITS AND THE INDIVIDUAL INVESTMENT DECISION

On an individual basis, there is a tendency to exaggerate the value of consumption benefits in adding to strictly measurable returns to education. They can serve as a convenient *deus ex machina* to explain a low calculated rate. The human spirit has an infinite capacity for rationalizing bad decisions.

Under the assumption that while individuals may make mistakes and miscalculations of their future earning power, the (*competitive*) market as a whole cannot, if the average measured rate for a given educational level fell below that on physical capital or if the rates for the same education investment in two fields differed, these differences would be attributable to consumption benefits. The reasoning seems like pure tautology, with rate differences serving as evidence of consumption benefit differences and consumption benefit differences explaining differences in rates. But this is not the case, under the assumption of rational choice and competitive market conditions which assume equal *total* (to include nonmonetary benefits) rates. Then consumption benefits act as a compensating residual.

The labor market behavior of male school teachers seems to suggest a case in which consumption benefits do not seem to play their compensating role. Their incomes from teaching are below those of others with a similar dollar investment in education; that is, their rate of return on education falls below the average. Consumption benefits can be examined as the sources of the relative weakness in their rates. The young man entering this field chooses teaching because he thinks he will like the career, giving him an opportunity to work closely with children and aid them through the complex process of mental development.

But if work-related consumption benefits are the answer, why do so many male school teachers moonlight? At almost 25 percent, their moonlighting rate far exceeds that of any other specific work group and is about five times the national average rate. Obviously, for many of these schoolteachers, *current* consumption benefits from teaching do not compensate for returns below those of their intellectual peers. They do not necessarily like teaching less than they thought they would at age eighteen, but it might be that at age thirty-six, for example, they value other things more—extras for a growing family, educated-middle-class consumption standards, all the things of the "good life" which money can buy. A Labor Department study of male teachers found the chief reason for moonlighting was not to meet the pressure of debts nor to cover temporary high expenses—moonlighting was a steady form of work life for those with two jobs—but simply to raise living standards.[2]

Tastes change with education and age. But don't the young know that their needs and economic priorities will vary as they get older? Many young people may try to plan ahead in line with what they think their future wants will be and choose careers accordingly. The clearest preference pattern eighteen-year-olds have, though, is their current one based on their present tastes, not on some future speculative schedule which they can see only through the haze of time not yet experienced.

Thus, as individuals, those at eighteen who choose to follow a teaching career may know all about low *average* measured rates of return and the telltale moonlighting rate for male schoolteachers. But for one thing, some will not believe that the average applies to them and think that they will do better. Adam Smith speaks of "the over-weening conceit which the greater part of men have of their own abilities," which he calls an "ancient evil." Even with a less sanguine view of their future earning power, many others preparing for the teaching field might feel that their own nonmonetary consumption benefits from teaching will raise their adjusted rate of return to the level attained by others with similar educational investment; moonlighting will not be for them.

[2] Harold W. Guthrie, "Teachers in the Moonlight," *Monthly Labor Review*, vol. 92, February 1969.

But it is a very weak theory that has market behavior dependent on collective misjudgment. While some who prepare for teaching over-estimate their future earning power and the value of *later* consumption benefits, we must assume that most do not, at least not to the degree that it influences them to undertake losing investments.

We must look for other reasons to explain the apparent labor market disequilibrium for male schoolteachers, manifested by their high moon-lighting rate. This involves a search for rationality in decision making that leads to a failure of consumption benefits to compensate for lower incomes during much of their work life.

Before examining the role of consumption benefits in this market further, we can look at another case in which there is *current* incom-plete compensation for income differences by consumption benefits. Within the academic field, consider the lower salaries and rates of return on educational investment received by humanities professors compared to science professors. In their study, Ashenfelter and Mooney find an internal rate of return of 8.6 percent for natural science professors, 5.3 percent for those in the social sciences, and a scant 0.7 percent for the humanities faculty—all who have invested in a Ph.D. after their B.A. Even the highest level is low by the standard of profitability we have established, but the issue here is over an explanation of the differential rate.

Ashenfelter and Mooney suggest that consumption benefits are a strong explanatory variable. They cite long vacations, stimulating colleagues, "idyllic geographical setting," and the "pure undiluted pleasure of stimulating young minds." But these psychic benefits accrue to the scientist just as much as to the humanist. As for their work itself, there is no reason to argue one way or the other as to who enjoys it more. While the humanist may delight in speculative reasoning based on argument and counterargument, the scientist derives pleasure from ab-stract thought. If intellectual effort thrives on the difficultly in finding irrefutable solutions to important questions, the scientist contemplat-ing the forces of nature or the origin of life faces just as much uncertain-ty and indeterminacy as the literary scholar weighing the influence of Ariosto on Cervantes.

In their explanation of why there are "literally thousands of grad-uate students in the humanities," who are preparing for careers as college teachers and "who probably have some idea of the low financial rewards which await them," Ashenfelter and Mooney call on consumption benefits as the factor giving rationality to their decision. They write, "There is probably something to this notion of large psychic benefits to an academician." But the science professor is also an academician.

Apparently, those who hold the view of superiority in nonmonetary benefits have not tried to convince the humanities faculty that their salary demands should be weaker than the pressure from the scientists because of their greater psychic income. In the absence of moonlighting data on college professors, we can assume that the humanists express their *current* market disequilibrium at least by dissatisfaction with their relative pay scales.

We can now try to explain why male schoolteachers moonlight, and why humanists grumble, within the framework of competitive markets with differential consumption benefits compensating for relative income and rate-of-return differences.

To some degree, though, the markets may not be competitive. For one thing, perhaps scientists form a noncompeting group—in the sense that the skills and aptitudes for science are confined to a small number, yielding scientists a return above the competitive rate that would prevail were entry unrestricted by an abilities barrier. Apart from such a hypothesis being more than mildly insulting to humanists, it could not realistically explain the vast differences in salaries and rates of return. Furthermore, it would most likely have no application to the schoolteacher case in that higher paying alternatives for them would not be outside their ability for investment in education.

We have previously discussed the lack-of-knowledge explanation of imperfection in these labor markets. Men do not flock into schoolteaching or into the humanities because they are unaware of the low earnings and less than compensating *future* consumption benefits that lie in wait for them.

The key to the explanation of how consumption benefits can play an equilibrating role, substantiating the two assumptions of rational choice and competitive labor markets, lies in the time pattern of these benefits. What is developed here for the case of male schoolteachers can be applied to the humanities example, *mutatis mutandis.*

If we consider that life's satisfactions are equally important whenever they occur, and acknowledge that consumption benefits unlike money cannot be stored, then the labor market behavior of male schoolteachers may be explained within the framework of rational decision making and perfectly competitive market conditions. At age eighteen the young man is eager to prepare for a teaching career, even given the knowledge of the low average returns to this career and of the high moonlighting rate. He looks forward to the psychic benefits of a secure position, absence of pressures associated with work in commerce and industry, the opportunity to develop young minds, etc. During his early years as a teacher, he enjoys these benefits (moonlighting typically does not begin until the thirties). Later his psychic benefits may pale, or his consumption wants become more pressing, but in any case his psychic returns no longer compensate for his low monetary earnings, and in these later years he either becomes disgruntled with his confined budget or he moonlights.

But the question here is whether or not he made an unwise decision. His tastes may change during his lifetime, but we must look at his life as a whole. If in the early years his strong consumption benefits more than compensated for his relatively low earnings, then, with an opposite attitude for the later years, who is to say that for his life as a whole he made an unwise decision? He cannot apply his unstable consumption benefits to his later years, but his lifetime total of these benefits may be sufficient to offset his relatively lower monetary internal rate of return. Under free choice, competitive labor markets, and rational decision making they would be.

Too often the words "You'll be sorry later for what you do now" forget the pleasures of what you do now or imply a greater weight to later satisfactions than to early ones. The above analysis, which gives equal weight to every year's satisfaction, denies Rabbi Ben Ezra's advice, "Grow old along with me, the best is yet to be, the last of life for which the first was made." To advise an eighteen-year-old youth to stay out of teaching, even though he has a strong preference for the career, because in later life his wants and attitudes will change has all the wisdom of counseling an equally young man to eschew radical politics because in thirty years he will become a solid member of the Establishment.

A final word of caution—because there may be some validity to the argument that strong early consumption benefits may counteract later weaker ones, there is no reason to believe that, on average, an exact equilibrium is reached. Where psychic returns and subjective evaluation play important roles, there is always the possibility of overestimating total lifetime consumption benefits. We do not want to assume that these benefits will always serve as a perfect residual market equilibrator, making, in accordance with perfectly competitive market conditions, every wage or internal rate-of-return difference exactly compensating. The uncertainty of subjective evaluation adds an element of imperfect knowledge to muddy the purity of competition. But at least the inclusion of lifetime rather than current consumption benefits in the analysis helps us understand the rationality in choice of careers that yield relatively low returns and less than compensating psychic benefits over part of the individual's work life.

SUMMARY

The individual faces a welter of confusing factors that make a rational educational investment decision difficult. Even if internal rates of return were accurately calculated, the average rate can only provide a rough guide to what he can expect from his own particular investment. At the outset of his schooling program he is not certain of his success in his school work—the quality of his investment—his ability to apply his investment to the most satisfying and best paying jobs, his later motivation to maximize his returns, and his good or bad fortune.

Being young, he might be very uncertain of his limitations and even of his long-run interests. But he pays a price for deferring his decision. If his true rate of return, including psychic benefits, lies above that of the adjusted rate on alternative investments, then each year he delays results in economic loss from these missed extra profits on educational investment.

In effect, the student makes a series of decisions regarding his investment, not just one at the beginning of a particular schooling level. He must decide whether to continue his course toward completion. Despite the high *average* rates for the last years of every schooling level, the pertinent issue to the individual student is whether the marginal rate of return on the remaining years for *him* exceeds the adjusted rate on alternative investments. The economically rational dropout is the student who figures that his marginal rate falls below the adjusted alternative rate. It does not matter that the rate he will earn on only partial schooling is low or that the marginal rate on the investment for the remaining years is higher; as long as this latter rate is below the comparable alternative rate, it pays for him to drop out.

The student, of course, considers psychic benefits in his choice of educational investment. But difficult as it may be, he should try to estimate his *total lifetime* consumption benefits from particular careers, counting the satisfaction of early years as heavily as those in later life. This reckoning can explain the choice of careers for which, on the average, at some later period a large number of workers find that low returns are not compensated by *current* consumption benefits, benefits which were higher for them years earlier.

The point of view of the individual is a personal one. He is interested in the benefits of education without concern over whether they result from improved productivity derived from education or from employer preference for educated workers or from some other source not related to productivity. On the other hand, the social investment decision, which we will now discuss, is vitally concerned with the basic source of returns to education.

CHAPTER SIX

The Public Investment Decision

Just as in the case of appraising the effectiveness of the internal rate of return as a guide to private educational investment decisions, it was found that conceptual uncertainties made even the simple rate difficult to calculate, with indirect and nonmonetary aspects further weakening the importance of the rate itself, so too, and even more so, is the social rate a shaky standard on which to base public policy decisions.

Further complications arise when we consider nonmonetary returns from education. Thus, when we say that the rate must be modified to include factors outside of direct costs and benefits, we really mean that these factors are to be taken into account in a nonquantifiable way in the investment decision, along with the rate, and not that the rate itself can be accurately adjusted to some new figure. In this context, minute refinement of the rate itself becomes a futile exercise in the pursuit of insignificant digits as long as the nonmeasurable factors have vague weights in the investment decision.

The special aspects of *social* nonmonetary factors that make them difficult to incorporate into educational investment policy are their breadth and instability. Previously we noted that our prevailing attitude toward economic growth may be in the process of change, from unqualified boon toward ominous threat to society's physical survival. If our view of such a tangible concept as economic growth can undergo such substantial changes over time, what can be said about the constancy of more abstract social values? The environment, brotherhood, international affairs, the war against poverty, and cancer all have their demands on the educational dollar; but what matters most for investment policy is that their relative importance varies over time as national interests and priorities change.

Tastes and interests for the individual student investors change too, and in the last chapter we argued that a lifetime view of consumption benefits could reconcile rational choice based on preferences at the outset and early years after investment with a later change in them. But what is the lifetime of a society? An investment made now in line with national interests, which becomes less valuable to society if these interests change in the near-term future, or even later, will be a losing one because the relevant time period for the investment will be the length of life of the physical facilities developed, which may be much longer than that of an individual's work life.

But decisions which will influence the long-term future direction of education must be made, despite the awareness of the decision makers that the factors with high values today may have less importance later on, and that current decisions thus might not yield the greatest social benefits. Admitting that decisions receive unclear signals from economic factors because of the immeasurability and variability of some of the policy variables, we fall back on the all-other-things-being-equal assumption, so useful to economic reasoning, and study decision making based on rate-of-return analysis in isolation. Even within these limitations conceptual difficulties arise which make policy recommendations uncertain.

Education raises national output, and we will assume society's welfare, if it increases productivity and if workers are paid in accordance with their productivity. If these earnings-productivity conditions are fulfilled, then it might seem that the calculated rate of return, based as it is on the equality of discounted earnings differences attributable to education and costs, will influence policy decisions on the direction and amount of educational investment. In this chapter, which focuses on the rate of return to the exclusion of nonmonetary factors, we will explain the uncertainties that arise for social investment policy even if both conditions are met—the tie of earnings to productivity and the contribution of education to productivity. Then, when the assumptions are relaxed, the rate of return loses even more of its force as a guide to a policy of investment efficiency.

MEASURING AND ALTERING THE ACTUAL
MARGINAL RATE OF RETURN

Not considering any factors other than measurable economic costs and benefits, society's welfare is maximized, and investment efficiency maintained, when rates of return are equalized on all public investment projects. The means by which equilibrium is reached whereby rate of returns are equalized for all investments are through application of funds to those projects for which the rate of return is the greatest. This principle applies within investment classifications as well as between them. Investment in a college would take precedence over a law school if the rate of return were higher for the former.

The feasibility of this simple policy prescription rests on the operation of marginal principles. Certain questions arise regarding the application of marginalism to educational investment decisions. Public investment decisions are characteristically lumpy. At issue is not the funding of a few students or purchase of a few pieces of equipment, but at least a whole college involving thousands of students, and sometimes an entire school system. Operation of marginal principles requires small changes in the application of resources to production, in this case schooling. How are decisions affected by lumpiness in public educational investment?

Rate-of-return studies yield only average rates, but marginal rates are the relevant ones for investment decisions. In competitive market equilibrium, marginal and average rates are equal, but does the market for college education fit the competitive framework?

Finally, with regard to following a policy of education for all through age eighteen, what steps should public authorities take to reduce the social cost of low returns if it discourages or prevents school leaving before high school completion? We now turn to these issues of public educational policy before relaxing the education-productivity-earnings assumptions.

The "Scale Effect"

Public investment decisions usually involve large amounts of additional costs applied to the production of significant increases in output. Thus, in education, we have the "scale effect" of the substantial change in the rate of return on investment in schooling if, say, in response to higher marginal rate on investment in college over alternative public investments, the community, state, or nation launches a heavy program of educational investment.[1]

All adjustments to the increase in schooling have a negative effect on the rate of return. With more young people in college, the supply of noncollege youths in the labor force declines, tending to raise their wages or the investment opportunity cost of foregone earnings. Pressures on existing facilities and instructional personnel may also raise the direct costs of schooling. Later on, the net returns from college will tend to decline as the supply of graduates increases. There may also be a later reduction in consumption benefits as the prestige of a college degree weakens with its wider attainment.

All this means that the public investment decision makers must take into account that when they expand education in response to the economic signal of a high marginal rate of return on such investments, they may overshoot the mark of bringing the rate down to the level of other investments by their application of funds to expand the level of schooling. It might be impractical to provide smaller doses of additional education in the attempt to obtain investment efficiency.

In reality, this problem of lumpiness of public educational investment is usually not too serious in that it just establishes a range of indeterminacy in investment decisions. If the marginal rate is substantially higher for college than for other investments, then the educational expansion can be undertaken with little fear that the rate will thereby be forced below that on other investments. Of course, if the current marginal rate on education is only a little above the level of other investments, then the decision on further educational investment becomes uncertain. But then the decision itself would be of minor importance as far as following the goal of investment efficiency is concerned, if rates of return on the range of possible public investments do not differ significantly.

Obviously, the range of indeterminacy equals the magnitude of the effect of the educational investment program on the internal rate of return. Not to minimize the damaging effect of lumpiness on clear-cut economic choice, if labor markets are somewhat insulated, even a local

[1] The term "scale effect" to refer to the jump in marginal values consequent to heavy investment in schooling was coined by Mary Jean Bowman, "The Costing of Human Resource Development," in G. E. A. Robinson and John Vaizey (eds.), *Conference on the Economics of Education*, Macmillan, 1966.

investment may have a substantial effect on the relevant rate. Ideally, the maximum deviation from uniform rates among alternative investments would equal one-half the change in the educational investment rate resulting from the "scale effect," assuming, and a heroic assumption it would be, that the size of the effect were known. If the smallest practical expansion in education in an area lowered the rate by 3 percent, then efficiency-maximizing policy of approaching equality in all rates would call for this expansion if the marginal rate on education were as little as 1 1/2 percent above the average rate on alternative investments.

A much more serious obstacle to rational public decision making than the jumpiness in the internal marginal rate of return is the uncertainty in the value of the *current* marginal rate itself.

The Marginal Rate of Return

Marginal analysis tells us that under competitive equilibrium, marginal and average values are equal. Therefore, at first view it might seem that though calculations can only yield estimates for average rates of return, these rates can be used as marginal values as well in decision making on educational investment.

The gist of the following argument is that such reasoning represents an erroneous extension of the conditions for competitive equilibrium in labor markets to earnings, or production, resulting from educational investment.

As for the labor market, although marginal analysis implies homogeneity or perfect interchangeability among the units of the factors involved, for example, welders, marginal principles are not deeply disturbed because there are variations in production efficiency among welders. We can use the *average* marginal value productivity as the value which will be equated with wages in competitive equilibrium.[2] Under the assumption of increasing, then decreasing, returns, this marginal productivity will first exceed the average productivity and then fall to that level at the number of welders hired, so that the average productivity itself will measure equilibrium wages. Then assuming a position of equilibrium of wages, employment, and marginal-average

---

[2]This method is suggested by Lester Thurow, *Investment in Human Capital*, Wadsworth, 1970.

productivity, the change in marginal productivity and wages from a small increase in employment of welders will be roughly equal to the measured level of average productivity.

But the crucial difference between welders and workers classified by a given educational level, say college graduates, is that the latter broad grouping cuts across occupational lines. This means that many individuals with the same education and investment costs will be spread out among many fields of work activity and, what is most important, will be at different earnings levels. These returns will, of course, differ widely between jobs, even if competitive conditions prevail *within* the individual occupational labor markets, whereby each worker receives more or less the marginal (value) product, and average equals marginal productivity.

The selection of work activity after education cannot be considered random. Assuming work choice is tied to quality of investment, those who get the most out of schooling will, of course, be in the higher paying fields. Their internal rate of return will be high, that is, above the average, and those who profit least from schooling will be in the lower paying jobs with below-average returns.

These last workers who receive competitive wages in their particular field of work will perhaps receive a rate of return on their investment below the adjusted rate on alternative investments. If such is the case, then it is not the market for the labor in question that is in disequilibrium, but rather there is an indication of overinvestment in college education.

If, for the moment, we ignore inequality in educational opportunity either because of discrimination or unavailability of investment funds— and there is nothing in this analysis that reduces the responsibliity of the state to equalize opportunity so that all receive the education they are capable of attaining—it is reasonable to assume that there is some order to the array of earnings derived from education. Individuals will make a conscious choice for a college education, based on economic considerations, if their expected rate of return from their schooling exceeds the rate on alternative investments. Of course, their estimation is subject to error, but it can be assumed that those with the greatest possibility for favorable returns will choose college easily. Those with less favorable prospects make a harder choice, and so on down the line. The low rates for some, especially those who earn below the average on such risky long-term investments, can be attributed to overly sanguine estimates of the profitability of college to them.

Those who do not opt for college, under the assumed condition of equality of opportunity and college costs, will be those with dim hopes for collegiate (financial) success, a conclusion strengthened by the general optimism of youth. Thus, if the state decides to expand education to raise the number attending college, the odds are that the marginal rate of return on this investment will be much below the current average level. For following the public investment efficiency policy, then, if the current calculated internal social rate of return, which is the *average* rate, based as it is on per student costs and mean or median earnings differences as the returns measure, lies above the adjusted alternative rate, this is by no means a valid signal for further educational investment to increase enrollment. In fine the (calculated) average rate is greater than the marginal rate. How much greater is uncertain, but the complication is serious enough to caution against indiscriminate use of the calculated rate as a guide to investment policy.

If we drop the unrealistic assumption of equality of opportunity, the public authorities should, on social efficiency grounds alone—to say nothing of equity—reach out to foster the education of those who would profit from schooling and who currently curtail their education because of lack of opportunity or resources. But this selective policy is quite different from one of blanket support on a random basis to those who do not currently attend college.

Compulsory Education and Dropout Policy

The above analysis is consistent with the conclusion of the last chapter that the typical dropout makes an economically rational decision in quitting school before completion because the rate *he* could earn on further investment in schooling would be well below the average, profitable rate. At the same time it was maintained that because of the social value of universal high school completion, social policy should discourage or, let us say more strongly, legally prevent dropping out of high school. These two positions must be reconciled.

This very policy, itself, would work wonders for the private rate of return. By eliminating individual choice and raising the compulsory school age to eighteen, foregone earnings would be wiped out for those between the present compulsory age, say sixteen, and eighteen years. Since presumably the state would back up its educational policy by providing full schooling up to this age, and in fact public high schools do that now so no adjustment would be required except an expansion of facilities, the private internal rate of return would be raised to infinity for all high school graduates. This, of course, assumes at least some improvement in earnings for the extra years in school.

But the rate-of-return gain from about 8 percent to infinity for the potential sixteen-year-old dropout who is forced to remain in school is a false measure of economic well-being. The student is better off than he would have been before the compulsory school age was raised only if the rate he could have earned from further schooling for the two years involved were greater than that on alternative investments—had he been allowed the choice to work and not been forced to continue school.

The fact that he wished to drop out indicates that this is not the case, and additional compulsory years of schooling impose a financial cost on him, even when the state provides free schooling (zero direct costs).

Here we see the conflict between private and social educational policy. The state decides to force expanded education for the non-monetary benefits derived even though this move involves an economic loss because of the low social rate of return, a rate much lower than the private one because the opportunity cost of direct investment in buildings, teachers, salaries, etc., are included in the social rate. But, even with free direct costs, the individual suffers a financial loss if the policy forces him to forego the choice of dropping out and going to work. The individual, in effect, is forced to pay for the social benefits of a more informed society, improved cultural environment, etc., which he personally may not value too highly. Even if he does, their total value is shared by all of society, and while the taxpayers as a whole pay for this uneconomic policy, his share of the costs is much greater than anyone else's.

But once the policy is decided upon, both the individual and society have the same goal—to try to raise the financial benefits to the affected students, those who would have otherwise dropped out of school.

One way to achieve this goal would be to reorder school curricula to suit the needs of the would-be dropout, by providing greater flexibility in course offerings for those who currently profit the least from a fixed pattern of academic subjects. Specifically, there needs to be more emphasis on vocational training for these crucial teen-age years. One study found a much greater stimulation to earnings from training over nondescript schooling for low achievers.[3] In the same vein, another study found a great financial loss from a dropout prevention program working within the existing school curriculum.[4]

Perhaps an improvement in training facilities and substitution of training for more formal academic schooling would raise the later earnings of those affected by the compulsory education policy enough to make their internal rate for the last two years of high school, with costs measured by former foregone earnings, higher than on alternative investments. Then, if the social rate were still lower than on other potential public investments, at least society as a whole would be paying for the nonmonetary benefits.

But what if, even with the best intentions and programs, the private rate were not raised enough to compensate for compliance with the program? (The same possibility arose with earlier legislation covering young children with compulsory education and child labor laws, and probably much of parental opposition to the latter was based on the economic loss involved.) The group affected is neither large nor politically powerful. Perhaps the state could simply let them grumble.

A more equitable treatment would provide payments for some part of maintenance costs while attending school. We do have living allowances with our government-operated training programs now, and there would be great advantages in training workers while they are young and still in school rather than later when they have already experienced failure in the world of work. Problems of administration would arise. Everyone would want to claim he was a potential dropout. Should only those who receive vocationally oriented education in their last years receive maintenance subsidies? Many a student at the margin of decision for future academic work would be pushed in a positive direction by a little reduction in his investment costs. But here we are entering issues in educational finance, the province of the last two chapters.

[3]W. Lee Hansen, Burton A. Weisbrod, and William J. Scanlon, "Schooling and Earnings of Low Achievers," *American Economic Review*, vol. 60, June 1970.
[4]Burton A. Weisbrod, "Preventing High-School Drop-outs," in Robert Dorfman (ed.), *Measuring Benefits of Government Investments*, The Brookings Institution, 1965.

PERSONAL CONTACTS, EDUCATIONAL
PREFERENCE, AND CREDENTIALISM

Education can lead to higher earnings, even if it does not increase productivity, but at the same time these higher earnings may be related to productivity. This simply means that educated workers may obtain higher-paying jobs which add much value to output, but that the aspect of education that opens these jobs to them has nothing to do with an improvement in their skills or in general development of their productive ability.

All this means that education plays favorites with the result that the educated get better jobs for which the lesser educated have the ability to hold but not the opportunity to obtain. The educated enjoy special privilege in the labor market because they make helpful personal contacts during their college years and because firms show a preference in employment for educated, college graduate workers.

Personal Contacts

If the higher earnings after college result from business contacts developed during college, these earnings should be included in calculating the private rate. From an individual point of view, although profitable personal relationships have nothing to do with learning, as long as they are made during schooling, the returns from them are no less tangible than those derived from study, and acquired knowledge and skills, and their later application to more productive higher-paying work.

Social benefits differ from private ones in that they include those derived by others as well as by those who receive the educational investment in question. But it should never be overlooked that they do include the benefits received by those directly involved. Thus, it might seem that society gains from the higher earnings of college graduates who get better jobs through personal contacts.

One important qualification, though, should be kept in mind. Benefits to individuals are net to society only if they are not at the expense of others. Accordingly, if a college graduate attains a high-paying job through contacts made at college, neither the direct returns nor work-related consumption benefits should be counted as social returns to education. Both types of advantages could have been enjoyed by the lesser educated worker who is deprived of the chance to compete for the job. Expressed differently, there is a good job available which could be filled adequately either by a college graduate or a lesser educated worker. That the college graduate gets the job adds nothing to total welfare—we avoid the utility quagmire—and reflects no social gain from education. There would be no loss in total output had the well-placed individual not attended college.

This conclusion is unaffected by the fact that decision makers on investment of public resources for college must accept and cannot change private customs and behavior whereby a financial plus through personal contacts falls to the college student. Thus, if public dollars are spent in college construction and staffing, that part of the average student's later earnings that issue from their college association rather than from learning are only at the expense of the high school graduate of equal productive capacity. These extra earnings related to college attendance should therefore be deducted in measuring social returns from college, thereby reducing the true internal rate of return.

Some public institutions focus on the education of lower-income students. Private returns will be less at these colleges where chances are slimmer for making financially profitable contacts than at higher-cost colleges where the few personable poor enrolled can gain from contacts made and the plentiful rich can feed on each other's opportunities. Social returns though, assuming equal training, are the same for both schools, when appropriate reductions for earnings unrelated to skills acquired and developed are deducted from the postcollege income of graduates of the expensive schools. In fact, the calculated rate for public colleges therefore gives a more accurate figure of the true social rate, and education planners would be advised to use calculated internal rates for public institutions only in the use of economic elements in their investment decisions.

Preference and Credentialism

Closely related to the extra earnings gained through college friends are the better jobs held by the college educated because of employer preference for college graduates. "Preference," in this sense, is defined as the use of a college degree in itself as a favorable attribute in firms' employment decisions—in hiring, promotion, etc.—without it having any real connection to ability in job performance. Preference of this nature can be called "credentialism," the consideration of the college diploma as a symbol of productive efficiency.

If preference is the shiny side of the coin, prejudice is its dirty side. What the college graduate gains by the discriminating use of the degree, the lesser educated, who could do the job as well, loses because of his (erroneously) implied inefficiency from the lack of a degree.

There is probably less social outcry against the credentialist than against the racist or sexist because, unlike the individual who suffers from these other forms of discrimination, the undereducated can cater to society's educational preferences and prejudices; he can go to college and get a degree. Two factors, though, make the problem a serious one. We do not have equality of educational opportunity, either because of financial barriers or the handicaps of prior poor schooling, with many suffering from both disadvantages. Secondly, even if college were equally available to all, think of the national waste if so much time and money were poured into activities that served no purpose other than to gratify the credentialist.

The extent of employer preference defies accurate measurement, but there is enough circumstantial evidence to suggest that we are not talking about a minor contributor to education-related earnings, but about a major offset to the true social rate of return. Hansen's study presents data for internal rates of return on various years of schooling.[5] For two years of college, he finds a social internal rate of only 5.4 percent. This rate is far below his assumed alternative rate of 10 percent and indicates that "some college" is a poor investment. On the other hand, his calculated rate for the last two years of college is a healthy 15.6 percent. The inference is clear; dropping out for the student who could finish with average earnings prospects is economically unwise, since the large returns of the last two years, which make the four-year program just profitable at 10.2 percent, are lost.[6]

But related to the issue of employer preference for college graduates, while Hansen himself does not speculate on the causes for the wide swings in marginal internal rates for the collegiate years, it seems reason-

[5]W. Lee Hansen, "Total and Private Rates of Return to Investment in Schooling," *Journal of Political Economy*, vol. 71, April 1963.
[6]Giora Hanoch, "An Economic Analysis of Earnings and Schooling," *Journal of Human Resources*, vol. 2, Summer 1967, finds a private rate of 7.1 percent for the first three years and 12.2 percent for the last years of college for Northern white students.

able to argue that not all the gain in returns for the last two years can be tied to great improvement in skills acquired and abilities developed during this period. Rather, the figures suggest that the diploma itself, to some extent, serves as an entrance ticket to the better jobs. If this view has any validity, then the true social rate for the last two years of college is lower than that calculated from college graduate earnings, unadjusted for the role of employer preference in these earnings.

Hansen's data on high school returns parallel the college figures, with low social returns for the first two years and much higher rates for the last two years, at 9.5 percent and 13.7 percent, respectively. Two years of high school do not involve such a heavy loss as two years of college, probably because high school costs are so much lower than college expenses, but the 9.5 percent rate still indicates an uneconomic investment. Again, on average, dropping out is a losing move, but a rational decision for many students in accordance with the argument of the last chapter that averages do not apply to individual students. Again, there is the suggestion that the high school diploma opens doors, not so wide as those through which the college degree gives passage, but still closed to high school dropouts.

Other data lend indirect support to the related thesis that increased education is not required for performing certain jobs or, expressed alternatively, that many occupations could be filled satisfactorily by those with less schooling. Over the past generation we have experienced a revolution in educational attainment, with the greatest relative gains in the high school years. We are fast approaching universal high school graduation.[7] Much has been said about the need for more schooling to satisfy today's and tomorrow's industrial demand for trained labor, and those who express this need take comfort in the thought that more and more schooling will not lead to excess supply of the educated but, in the best tradition of economic rationality, will only represent an equilibrating adjustment to burgeoning demand. The data, though, question this description of economic harmony. In fact, the figures below on the trend of educational attainment for various occupations support a contrary position—that some of our workers are becoming overeducated for the jobs they hold.

---

[7] The percentage of the work force with at least a high school diploma increased from 43 to 67 percent over the period 1952-1971 (while median years of school completed rose from 10.9 to 12.4). See *Manpower Report of the President*, 1972.

Table 6-1 shows the trend over the past twenty-five years for two high-earnings groups—professionals and managers—and for lower-income, lesser-educated groups—those in industry and the broad class of service workers. Professionals, with their exacting preparation, have always required a high level of education. The managerial group has had a rather stagnant average level of schooling which in fact has fallen, relatively, to a present level very close to the all-occupation average.

Most interesting, though, has been the schooling experience at the lower end of the occupational scale. While the overused statement about industry's needs for a more educated work force may apply to craftsmen and especially foremen, making for a parallel growth in demand and supply of educated workers, can the same be said for operators, laborers, and service workers? From an educational level a little beyond grade school, they are now, on average, approaching the high school graduate status. Perhaps industry's tasks are more complex, but we can certainly question whether the figures which reveal the revolution in educational attainment would be matched by a similar (unavailable) table of employment educational needs. Put more specifically, if a sweeper could perform his job with little more than an eighth-grade education twenty-five years ago, would his duties have become so much more intricate that he would need to have almost a high school diploma today?

TABLE 6-1

*Median years of school completed by the
employed civilian labor force
18 years and over
selected occupation groups and dates
(1948-1971)**

Occupation group	1971	1966	1962	1957	1952	1948
Professional and technical workers	16.3	16.3	16.2	16 +	16 +	16 +
Managers, officials, and proprietors	12.8	12.6	12.5	12.4	12.2	12.2
Craftsmen and foremen	12.2	11.9	11.2	10.5	10.1	9.7
Operators	11.4	10.7	10.1	9.5	9.1	9.1
Nonfarm laborers	11.1	9.5	8.9	8.5	8.3	8.0
Service workers	11.9	10.9	10.2	9.0	8.8	8.7
All occupation groups	12.4	12.3	12.1	11.7	10.9	10.6

*Source: *Manpower Report of the President,* 1972.

Let us examine the significance of a negative answer to this question, which could be applied to many other unskilled jobs. From the strictly economic point of view, when workers are overeducated for their job duties, earnings from these jobs cannot be attributed to this extra education. Therefore, if a sweeper with twelve years of schooling does work that could be performed with an eighth-grade education, there is no social return related to this work for the extra four years of education. There would be private returns if a high school diploma is made an arbitrary job requirement unrelated to skill, but as before, the social rate of return must be written down to the extent that higher earnings from better jobs reflect employer preference for educated workers rather than payment for skills actually developed by schooling.

In the cases under question the issue is not so much over preference for a high level of education in hiring for better jobs, since only the lower-echelon jobs are being considered, but of more than enough education to satisfy actual job requirements. The contribution to the private rate of return from extra schooling for these jobs would also be zero, since those with lesser education would have the same earnings; but, pertinent to the current discussion, the social rate for overeducation for job duties is zero, whether the extra schooling applies to the better paying jobs not open to capable workers with less schooling or to lower rated work which the educated and lesser educated both perform.

The humanist might chafe and rebel at this whole analysis. To a careless observer it might seem to lead to the dreary conclusion that much of the educational revolution has been a national waste, using funds and resources that would have been more productively applied to other public investments. We are moving, though, full circle to the book's opening defense of study of economic aspects of human capital investments.

All the analysis says is that when jobs held by some with a given level of education could be filled by those with lesser schooling, there are no (social) economic returns from the extra schooling. In fact, as we move toward universal high school graduation, there will be still more jobs for which the worker's educational attainment exceeds job requirements. But it is one thing to claim that workers are over-educated for job duties and quite another to argue that they are over-educated. The economist acknowledges the social value of the educational goal of universal high school completion. He does not worry that the economic returns from more and more generalized schooling tend to fall as the overall demand for acquired skills lags behind supply. Noneconomic factors may easily outweigh dollar-and-cents considerations in case the offset to net earnings of the educated that should be made if their higher incomes are not all attributable to greater productivity acquired through schooling lowers the social rate of return below that on other state investments.

Finally, the economist might wonder why the humanist fears a finding of low returns. Has he such little confidence in the other attributes of schooling, or in the decision makers' strong interest in them? Quiet reason suggests that the nonmonetary virtues of formal learning, at least through high school for all, do not need the added support of bad logic and consequent faulty figures.

But there are unfavorable aspects of overeducation for work and related credentialism even to those receiving the benefits of preference. These days we hear much talk of "worker alienation," dissatisfaction with the monotonous routine of jobs for which workers are educationally overqualified. As a solution to this problem, a recent article suggests that business will have to build more satisfaction into lower-echelon jobs and that educated workers will have to modify their career aspirations to derive contentment from less important jobs than they had hoped to fill.[8]

If these efforts are successful, "worker alienation" will be soothed, but at the same time credentialism would be extended as the increased number of degree holders pressed ever downward along the occupational ladder, pushing the hapless lesser educated but equally qualified still lower. In a stinging attack on credentialism, Berg noted an increased tendency to use education as an employment screening device in line with the increase in educational attainment, but he found no evidence of superior work performance by the educated for a number of different specific occupations and work classifications.[9] He concludes that increasing credentialism simply exacerbates the employment problems of the educationally disadvantaged who face still another barrier to equal employment opportunity.

In a similar vein, Thurow claims that our labor markets have become more and more characterized by job competition, with a range of jobs needing to be filled and education serving as entry to the better ones for which actual skill development is derived from on-the-job training

[8]"The Job Gap for College Graduates in the 1960's." *Business Week*, September 23, 1972.
[9]Ivan Berg, *Education and Jobs: The Great Training Robbery*, Praeger, 1970.

rather than from formal schooling.[10]   The result of this practice has been to exert a tightening squeeze on the lesser educated as the greater number of college graduates push them to ever lower-paying jobs; from 1949 to 1969 the median income of college graduates rose from 124 to 137 percent of the high school level, while in reaching for lower-level jobs, their income fell from 148 to 144 percent of the national average. Thus a steady rate of return on college may partly reflect the relatively lower earning capacity of the lesser educated who suffer from the discrimination of credentialism.

If, as all the evidence points, employer preference, or credentialism, is on the rise, unfortunately the market checks to this tendency are rather weak. Those who worry about excessive schooling often resort to strong figurative language in describing our colleges and universities as "grinding out" or "spewing forth" graduates.

The analogy of a college as an intermediate parts manufacturer shaping raw material (students) for producers of finished products (the labor market) simply will not hold. A manufacturer receives his production signals from his purchasers, and if the final producer reduces his demand for parts, the supplier cuts back his production. But the college is under no immediate pressure to cut back its production (enrollment) in the face of declining labor market demand for graduates. In the main, it is the raw material (students) who must look past the intermediate colleges to make their collegiate investment decision, and as long as credentialism persists, they are under less economic pressure to reduce this investment.

It might be too much to ask of private colleges and universities to combat credentialism by limiting or even reducing enrollment, considering that they are having financial difficulties, that graduates themselves do not lose out by employer preference, and, especially, that preference may be strongest for private college graduates.

Then shouldn't the public college be in a better position to blunt credentialism by reducing investment to the degree that college does not add to productivity? After all, public colleges receive their main financial support from taxpayers who can respond by holding back funds to that part of college investment which adds nothing to total output. The prescription is simple enough, but works to the detriment

[10]Lester Thurow, "Education and Economic Equality," *Public Interest*, vol. 28, Summer 1972.

of the poorer students who need this state subsidization, without which they will suffer from the discriminatory side of credentialism, adding still another handicap to their struggle toward earnings equality.

A serious problem in public educational policy has developed. To limit investment in schooling because the true social return is lower than that calculated by reason of employer preference would aid public investment efficiency but would handicap those who depend on public higher education. To ignore the effect of credentialism on the rate of return or, more strongly, even to expand public facilities so that educational opportunity is widened and the number suffering from the absence of a degree reduced would not only be costly, but socially damaging in addition, because the remaining lesser educated would be crammed even further down at the bottom of the occupational ladder. At the limit we would eliminate credentialism by a policy of universal college graduation.

Credentialism exists, and public authorities must adjust their investment decisions to this fact of (business) life. As a practical matter, given budgetary constraints, even governmental units will have to make their own adjustment decision based on the tradeoff between investment efficiency and equalization of earnings opportunities.

CONSPICUOUS PRODUCTION

In his insightful essay on the economics of education, Bowen introduces the apt term "conspicuous production" to describe the practice of many firms of preferential hiring of college graduates.[11] Bowen's implied definition of preference is even stronger than that presented here—of giving precedence to college graduates for particular jobs over equally qualified lesser-educated applicants, with the degree serving as a symbolic promise of future production excellence.

Bowen also has in mind the circumstance in which the college graduate also receives higher pay rates ("college graduate" salaries he calls them) than would be received by the lesser educated in the absence of college-preference. In this sense, Bowen's term conceptually closely follows Veblen's earlier expression "conspicuous consumption." Veblen

[11] William G. Bowen, *Economic Aspects of Education*, Princeton University Press, 1964.

referred to those consumer expenses which gave the buyer the psychological satisfaction of manifest demonstration of wealth—purchases of ostentatious luxuries or time-consuming activities—apart from the intrinsic physical utility of these goods and services. Similarly when a firm engages in "conspicuous production," it receives not only the workers' output for the wages it pays but also the self-satisfying feeling of prestige at having college graduates in its work force. It pays for the latter benefit in a wage higher than the worker's contribution to output, his marginal product.

We have no way of measuring the extent of "conspicuous production." Hansen's figures, or method, on incremental returns for various years of schooling will not help because the higher returns to college graduates may be partly attributable to employer preference as well as to conspicuous production.

For the sake of comprehensive coverage of the conceptual issues involved, let us assume that "conspicuous production" is more than a theoretical fiction—it is an actual description of employment practices of many firms.[12] To analyze the effect on returns to education, we must assume that the psychological benefits accrue only to the firms themselves. If its customers also prefer to deal with firms that use college graduates for particular jobs, then they derive a form of consumption benefit from their purchases. Take the case of a drug firm that employs only college graduate salesmen. Their representatives may enjoy easier entry into hospitals and doctors' offices than those of firms with less rigorous educational requirements. Fortunately, the question of consumption benefits of purchasers raises no special problems. If they exist, then the marginal (value) product of the worker will be consequently raised, and "conspicuous production" will tend to disappear, or, more accurately, the residual will represent the satisfaction derived by the hiring firm itself, the basic element in the term.

Looking at the private rate first, the same conclusion is reached as that regarding all factors that affect income related to school attainment. All earnings so realized are included in the private return, and no

---

[12]M. Blaug, "The Rate of Return on Investment in Great Britain," *The Manchester School*, vol. 33, 1967, for example, questions whether a large number of firms actually pay workers more than they are worth for reasons of prestige. He writes, "But is it reasonable to believe that industry would waste £300 to £500 per worker on a quarter of a million people?" We can ask, though, if the practice provides consumption benefits, is it really a "waste"?

tortured adjustment must be made because the earnings attributable to schooling are not all the result of developed skills and trained intellect. If the firm wants to pay more than the college graduate is worth, the happy recipient asks no questions and counts the money as part of his deferred returns to four years of college.

For the complicated issue of the effect on social returns of "conspicuous production," payment above the college-trained worker's marginal value product, it is easier to break the analysis into two parts—the first in which the firm takes the extra cost of the above competitive wages in the form of reduced profits, and the second with the firm passing the cost on to product purchasers in higher price. In the first case, the firm pays for its own consumption benefits. We could stretch marginal-productivity theory to put a money value on the psychic satisfaction of having college graduate employees, and with this adjustment, marginal costs would not be out of line with marginal revenue. The firm would be a satisfaction maximizer if not a profit maximizer.

Marginal-productivity theory, though, shows reluctance to include nonmonetary elements in its analysis. For one thing, it tries to predict behavior of the individual firm, and if a more complex goal than profit maximization is postulated, it becomes difficult or impossible to judge the firm's employment-output-pricing policies. But rate-of-return-on-human-investment analysis has a more macroeconomic orientation, especially for the social rate. The extra earnings resulting from "conspicuous production" should be included in social returns to education because there is a net gain to society from these higher earnings, if not in improved productivity of the workers involved, in consumption benefits of the firms—to their stockholders or management or both.

There should be no confusion between this tentative reasoning and the treatment of the returns to simple preference, which case included the tacit assumption that a college degree was used as an inappropriate proxy for an objective measurement of differential ability, and gave the holder no superior sentimental attraction to the employer. Thus, in the case of simple job preference, the earnings of the college graduate were at the expense of a qualified "uncertified" worker, with an assumed neutral effect on total welfare.

A numerical example might help clarify the adjustments to be made when "conspicuous production" is added on to simple preference; and the former only arises, as a supplement to the latter, because there is no prestige value in employment of college graduates for work which requires a degree for its satisfactory performance. If the marginal revenue for a certain job is $190 per week and the college graduate receives $200 for this work which could be done by lesser-educated workers who hold jobs that pay only $160 per week, then the net social returns from the job, the value of the consumption benefits to the firm, which it "buys" from the graduate employee, would be $10, not the $40 surplus in earnings over the lesser-educated earnings level. This calculation assumes a neutral welfare effect of the $30 gain to the college graduate and $30 loss to those who do not hold the degree from not getting a $190 job for which they are qualified.

Similarly, for the second case of "conspicuous production," in which the firm passes the extra cost of above-competitive wage on to product purchasers, in higher prices, there is still a small net social return from the practice. Under this condition, wages will no longer exceed marginal value product because of the price rise; but in effect, the consumer pays for the firm's consumption benefits, since the dollar value of output of college graduates now exceeds its real contribution.

Returning to the numerical example we can assemble all the welfare changes and assumptions involved. The college-trained worker receives $10 more than his economic value to the employer, which also measures the consumption benefits to the firm. He would receive $30 more than the high school graduate, in the absence of "conspicuous production," and the two welfare changes related to this $30 are assumed to cancel each other out. The public pays $10 more for the good produced than its real value, measured in previous dollars, and the welfare loss to the public of financing the firm's consumption benefits is assumed to equal the utility of the $10 extra earned by the college workers. The net adjustment of all these changes in earnings and assumed welfare valuations is a $10 social return on investment in schooling, the estimated money worth of the firm's consumption benefits.

The econometrician, who wants to find a clear value or limiting range for the social rate of return, might throw his hands up in disgust at the above analysis with its hodgepodge of nonmeasurable variables—qualitative but unquantifiable pluses and minuses of consumption benefits, "conspicuous production," preference and welfare assumptions—which only add to the confusion of all the other imponderables that prevent orderly calculation of rates of return. To him we offer our sincere regrets, but conceptual uncertainties cannot be ignored if the calculated rate of return is to have any respect as a useful decision-making tool in the important policy area of public educational investment.

SUMMARY

Nonmonetary elements complicate public educational investment decisions much more than private ones because changing social interests and priorities operate within a framework of the indefinite life-span of a society. But even if we limit our consideration to the rate of return itself, as was done in this chapter, problems arise in estimating the actual rate that should be used for public decisions based on investment efficiency—the equalization of marginal rates of return on all public investments.

The "scale effect" of large educational investments introduces a discontinuity in the marginal rate. In addition, calculated estimates are only of the average rate of return, and it is the marginal rate that is relevant for policy. The latter is smaller than the former, even under conditions of labor market competition, and the unknown magnitude of this difference makes economically rational investment decision difficult. If society follows a policy of universal high school graduation and raises the compulsory schooling age to eighteen, then it must try to raise the rate of return for the would-be dropout for his last years of schooling. A stronger focus on vocational training during school years would help, but if the improved rate still made the extra years an unprofitable investment, equity suggests some means of subsidization to the affected students to avoid having them pay more than their share for the whole society's benefits from this extra schooling.

Even if wages are tied to productivity, the calculated rate overstates social returns to educational investment if higher earnings for the educated result from features of schooling not related to an improvement in productive ability. Personal contacts made at college and employer preference for degree recipients—credentialism—contribute to earnings of the educated, without adding to total output.

Besides lowering the true social rate of return below the calculated level, credentialism has harmful effects on those who do not receive a high level of schooling, as employer preference for the educated keeps pace with the expansion in educational attainment. Those who benefit from employer preference for the educated also suffer from "worker alienation" as they fill jobs which demand less ability than their schooling has developed. Correct social policy to deal with credentialism has its uncertainties. On the one hand to invest further in schooling involves a waste of resources if this added education does not contribute to output, but on the other hand, failure to do so adds another difficulty in the path of opportunity for higher earnings of the poorer students dependent on public subsidization for their education.

"Conspicuous production," the payment of higher wages to college graduates because of the satisfaction the firm derives from having an educated work staff, may not be a large component of college graduate earnings. But to the extent firms reduce profits or pass on the cost to consumers in higher prices, these consumption benefits are a net contributor to social welfare, with other associated gains and losses canceling out.

CHAPTER SEVEN

Financing Education– Early Schooling

Public policy in education deals with decisions regarding the source of investment funds and their expenditures. Questions of equity and efficiency arise in both these aspects of government policy. Unfortunately, the goals are often in conflict. For example, if equity demands the same expenditure per student, then efficiency will not be served if some students are able to learn and earn more from the same dollar investment, since efficiency (total returns) could be raised by transfer of funds from the less to the more able. If the equity goal is equal returns from each student, using differential educational investment as an economic income- and welfare-equalizing drive, then obviously the efficiency goal would be even further neglected as much more money would be directed to the less able to equalize the results of their schooling with the lightly invested apt students.

A way out of the problem of matching the two goals is found by giving primacy to equity considerations. Then once the equity goal is set, efficiency becomes simply a matter of attaining equity with a minimum of resources. This does not mean that there cannot be vigorous dispute over what should constitute the equity goal. But suppose that the equity standard calls for equal educational investment for all students, then efficiency is obtained by spending the money in the most suitable (profitable) way for the individual students. As was discussed in the previous chapter, if investment for all is to be applied through high school years, then on efficiency grounds, some investment should be made for early vocational education as well as in conventional academic schooling. Both private and social returns are increased by this efficient practice.

This chapter deals with the equity and efficiency aspects of both parts of lower-education financing—the getting and spending of public funds on educational investment—the next, with higher education financing. What may be called the underlying equity principle for early schooling, the basic provision, over which there is little quarrel, is that the state should provide for every student the resources for universal education through the compulsory school years. We have argued for lifting this age through high school completion or its training equivalent, but this is not the place to quibble over the value of a year or two more of schooling.

It is not the element of compulsion that requires state financing. The state demands a great deal of compliance from each of us with what it determines as social needs, while making us pay for it ourselves in money or foregone leisure. Auto inspection, dog licensing and inoculation, and sidewalk snow removal cost us time and money to satisfy community regulations; albeit this cost is much below that of a high school education.

When we also deny that the primary reason for state financing of (high school) education is that society gains by this level of schooling for all, we do enter an area of controversy. Especially since the social benefits of an educated population were stressed in the earlier analysis, it might seem logical to argue that the state needed to support education to assure the attainment of the minimum level of schooling that would guarantee these benefits. But while the social benefits are important, it is really the positive returns from high school-level education we think should be enjoyed by everyone that obliges the state to finance education.

There is really nothing new in state provision of services vital to the individual. Some public health activities, for treatment of communicable and mental diseases, for example, have strong social overtones. But even these services are of crucial importance to the patients themselves. Public hospitals for noncommunicable ailments, or treatment of injuries, are certainly conducted almost exclusively for the benefit of the patients.

But in the health field, public financing is mostly limited to those who cannot finance the services themselves that society feels should be available to all regardless of ability to pay. For the most part, the solvent ailing pay for private medicine.

Public education, on the other hand, finances the schooling not only of those with insufficient means but also of many children whose families can and do finance their schooling through tax payments. Thus, while the essentiality of education requires that the state provide schooling for those who cannot pay for their own schooling, it is not enough to justify the need for a fully developed public school system. While there are many who do attend private schools, the bulk of the population receives its education through schools that are publicly financed and administered. The implicit assumption of the current system, then, holds that there are intrinsic social benefits from public education itself, and that even if all could finance their schooling costs, public education should be maintained because of its special benefits to society.

Currently there is growing criticism of the efficiency of public education. Many question the need for the special support public schools receive or, more accurately, the severe financial handicaps under which private schools must operate in competition with public institutions. They imply there are no special benefits inherent in a public system. Still others doubt that the method of financing public education satisfies minimum educational needs equitably. They feel that the equity principle should be extended to entail not just the same years of schooling for all but the same quality of education, with quality measured mainly by dollar amount of investment.

THE EXISTING SYSTEM OF
FINANCING EARLY SCHOOLING

Before examining these two criticisms of the existing system—the latter dealing with its equity in financing and the former with financing and related administrative efficiency—it is in order to describe just what is under criticism, that is, the current methods of early education financing and administration.

Public schools are financed at the community level by taxes, mainly on property. Presumably, within each local government unit, each school is allocated roughly equal funds for education so that each pupil covered by the local tax system receives about the same investment per school year.

But there are vast differences among communities in their wealth, or property tax base, and less but substantial variation in their willingness to pay for public education—measured by their tax rate. Since the wealth factor dominates, the wealthier communities, those with the higher valued property, invest more per child than the poorer localities, in which often the tax rate is higher.

Since tax revenues for education are based on property valuation and not on the number of children attending public schools, the family with no children contributes as much to the community public schools as another with the same property valuation having any number of children at school. Similarly, those parents who choose to have their children educated privately support the public school system to the same extent as those whose children attend the public schools. Thus, the choice for a private education becomes an expensive one indeed, with the parent having to pay almost the same tax for support of the public school system as if his child went to the public school, in addition to the considerable outlay he must make for private school education. He pays not quite as much in taxes because the withdrawal of his child from the public schools reduces their total operating costs. For the single taxpayer-parent, the saving amounts to very little since the reduction in total costs is shared equally among all parents, including those of the rest of the students who remain in the public schools. Of course, if there were a mass movement to private schools, then the tax saving would become substantial and, under the present method of financing, would again be shared equally by families with children who stayed in the system and those who left.

Public schools are not only financed through tax funds but are also administered by public bodies—school boards which decide on all phases of school operation within the budget allocated from taxes by local government. These boards decide on teachers' salaries, although the trend is for their decision to become less unilateral and more the result of collective bargaining. They also decide on material, equipment, and construction expenses and their allocation among schools within their jurisdiction.

Although the above description of the existing system is very simplified and thin, it does provide a background for discussion of current criticisms of it. Attacks on inequity of the system center around arguments against the property tax as a basis of public school financing. Attacks on its inefficiency offer substitute plans for financing, and especially for administration. These plans also have equity implications and are based on disagreement with the implied assumption that public schools provide special social benefits which justify their preferred financial treatment.

THE PROPERTY TAX CONTROVERSY

That the system of financing public schools results in much more spent per pupil in wealthier than in poorer districts has always been recognized. In addition, there have been efforts, feeble to be sure, to move toward greater equality through small amounts of federal funding for the most obviously underinvested children and through state reapportionment of taxes to poorer school districts. Nevertheless, until very recently, the amount invested per child, and presumably the quality of his education, varied with the value of the property in his district, which in turn depended on the wealth of his family and neighbors, and the industrial accident of the presence or absence of highly assessed commercial property in his tax district.

Challenges to this financing system have been consistent with the growth of equalitarian sentiment in the country. In its historic 1954 antisegregation decision of *Brown v. Board of Education,* the Supreme Court held that separate was not equal and that therefore racial segregation in education discriminated against blacks in educational opportunity, violating individual rights of equal protection under the law guaranteed by the Fourteenth Amendment. As a logical extension of this decision, many people argued that the Court was really striking down all forms of discrimination in education, and since wealth differences clearly discriminate against the quality of education received by the poor under the present system, that system should be declared un-

unconstitutional. To argue against the point that the wealthy have advantages in many areas—in the quantity and quality of products they buy and in the variety and scope of their leisure-time activities—opponents of the property tax as the basis of educational finance maintain that quality education, at least for early schooling, is a basic right of all, without condition based on economic circumstances. In legal terminology they view good (equal) schooling of "fundamental interest" to the individual student, an interest which is clearly not served by a program that determines investment per child on the local property tax.

There is nothing new in considering wealth a discriminating determinant where fundamental interest is involved. The poll tax was banned on just that basis. Similarly in ordering reapportionment of voting districts in line with population densities, the Supreme Court held that voting power should not be determined by location of residence, if the rights of individuals to equal protection under the law are to be upheld.

Combining these two views, the California Supreme Court, in what promises to be a far-reaching decision, declared the (typical) California system of property tax financing of public education unconstitutional. In judging that the system violated the "fundamental interest" of pupils in equal education, it argued that "if a voter's address may not determine the weight to which his ballot is entitled, surely it should not determine the quality of his child's education."[1]

Let us play devil's advocate awhile and attack the logic of the decision from the negative point of view of a well-to-do resident of a high-expenditure per pupil school district. There is no sense denying that his narrow self-interest is not served by the California verdict.

To him, the basis of the California court's decision involves a complete *non sequitur*. Of course, people should not be discriminated against in voting by their lack of financial resources or because of their residence in a particular area. But to extend this doctrine to require even quality in education is to ban wealth as a determinant of future earning power and basis for enjoying "the good life." A child's address is no accident but is greatly dependent on his family's income.

---

[1]For a clear, if perhpas one-sided discussion of this decision in the case *Serrano v. Priest*, see the article "Financing Schools: Property Tax Obsolete," *The Saturday Review*, November 20, 1971. Other states have since followed the California example, and the U.S. Supreme Court will probably soon decide on the constitutionality of the property tax as a basis for school funding.

Some *minimum* level of schooling should be provided to everyone in order to satisfy "fundamental interest" and to provide society with the benefits from universal education for good citizenship. But to deny the extra returns from greater investment that will accrue to the student himself, either in higher earnings or greater private consumption benefits, would be tantamount to denying wealthy investors the return from their physical capital investment. The bulk of returns to schooling, even at the early level, falls to the recipient of the investment and, in keeping with old-fashioned capitalistic economic principles, should be mainly retained by the investor. In keeping, too, with support of the progressive tax philosophy, the student will pay relatively higher income taxes on his greater earnings in later life, just as heavy recipients of physical capital interest and dividends are conditioned to pay higher tax rates. High property taxes, if admittedly not high rates, paid by the wealthier districts and existing, admittedly drastically incomplete, state equalization formulas will assure a minimum education level for all sufficient to satisfy individual "fundamental interest" in schooling and society's needs for an informed electorate. Anything more than this in the way of having the rich finance the education of the poor would be nothing less than a giant income redistribution scheme in which those who had accumulated capital and were able to invest it in their children were asked to share it with those with paltry capital stocks.

An economically sophisticated wealthy disputant might give a little ground at this point. He would recognize that this capital transfer to his children in the form of educational investment could be construed as a taxable gift or, even more logically, as a prepaid legacy, given in the donor's lifetime. To the extent parents invest in their children's education, they give them an earning asset, intangible and uncertain in value though it may be, which in effect reduces their inherited wealth in the more conventional assets of money and property. Consideration of the capital nature of educational expenditures might lead the wealthy to agree that above-average investment in schooling might be subject to an additional redistributive levy, in the form of a prepaid inheritance tax.

But they would not concede more than this. In summary, then, the position of the defender of the property tax, although it may not for political reasons be expressed so bluntly, admits that students in districts which collect a large amount of property taxes will receive a more expensive (better) education. They do not consider this advantage a geographical accident, but the result of having the good fortune to be born in high-income families who live in expensive housing and who are eager to use the value of their property as a basis for investing heavily in their children's education. This schooling will yield great financial returns in later life, but so would a legacy of $20,000; and except for gift and inheritance taxes, our system does nothing to deter the latter transfer.

This argument, strong though it appears when devoid of the cant and soft language required for its political presentation, has its economic rebuttal. Although the differential returns from early education related to variation in quality of schooling are difficult to measure, they are certainly very high. Undoubtedly, the source of the greatest part of these extra gains is in the option value of the high school diploma in obtaining a profitable college education. If schooling of those who received higher early investment stopped after high school, they probably would not earn much more as recipients of quality high school education than those with an inferior early schooling. This is especially true for the future when occupational opportunities for those with no college, whatever the quality of their high school education, will be even more tightly limited. Of course, there will be extra consumption benefits in being educated for those who go to high schools having Olympic swimming pools and cafeterias with a Rathskeller atmosphere, even if there is no financial payoff for these amenities.

But the percentage of graduates from these schools who receive preparation that will lead to a college education is higher than for graduates who receive low investment in high school. What is more, the chances are greater that they will go to colleges which will provide a profitable education. Profitability refers to the broadened meaning of the word to include consumption benefits as well as the financial returns from higher earnings. From a societal view, the former takes on added significance. As we tend to demand a college degree as a minimum requirement for important positions, and the more prestigious the college the more valued the degree, we in effect ban those without this symbol of academic achievement from interesting and responsible work in business and even politics. Thus, the poor are severely handicapped from ever attaining positions of leadership.

Translating this into economic terms, this aspect of consumption benefits simply adds further to the high returns from expensive early schooling. So far, though, nothing special has detracted from the strength of the status quo property tax argument. But the case against the property tax becomes convincing if, as is undoubtedly the case, the average rate of return on quality early schooling is high, specifically, higher than on alternative investments.

Capital market imperfections prevent poor students from funding a quality early education, that is, of taking advantage of the high returns available. They are discriminated against, not by the wealthy, but by their poverty and their consequent inability to purchase good schooling with borrowed funds.

In short, the present system discriminates economically against the poor. They cannot take advantage of the opportunity for the higher earnings, power, and prestige that good schooling brings. They are condemned for life to second-rate jobs and second-class citizenship by their inability to finance a better education. Not to overstate the case, the degree of economic discrimination is roughly measured not by the difference in average rates of return from schooling between those who have a great deal invested in them and those who have only a little, but the difference between the rate for the affluent and the average rate on alternative investments. This is the monopolistic advantage accruing to the rich, not because of their discriminatory practices, but because of imperfection in the capital market. The difference that might arise between average rates of return on investments as a whole and on that of investment in education of poorer students may be attributable to other forms of discrimination, mainly in employment. Biases against people obviously lower returns on embodied human capital.

That the poor suffer many other forms of economic discrimination is no argument for discrimination in returns from education. If more were invested in the poor or, put differently, if investment per student were equalized, and all other factors such as postschooling opportunities, ability, motivation, for examples, were equal, the rate of return on early schooling for the wealthy would fall until, under competitive equilibrium, rates of return on all investments were the same. The rich might not like this loss of their monopolistic advantage, but the maintenance of returns to privilege is poor justification for retention of the property tax.

Those who show little faith in the market argue that raising expenditures per pupil, mainly in the form of teacher salaries, would not improve education nor raise returns of what are assumed to be underinvested students, but would only overpay inferior instruction. Apart from the possibility of directing added investment to nonlabor instructional inputs—better buildings, classrooms, and equipment—certainly, over time, better teachers would be attracted by higher salaries.

Much more serious are findings that differences in academic results may not be closely associated with the greater expenses per pupil in high-property value areas but to the income and social status of the families themselves.[2] The implication here is that the higher returns for the students in the wealthier neighborhoods are not related to increased productivity and could not be captured by increase in expenditures on poorer students—added money that could only affect direct returns through improvement of the quality of the educational product. Differential indirect returns to the wealthy of family background, better job contacts, and job preference would remain. These studies, though, must be inconclusive as long as there are so few serious attempts to invest heavily in the education of the underprivileged.

The California decision says nothing about the means of equalizing educational opportunity. It merely states that the present property tax method handicaps the poor. The simplest interpretation of the intention of the verdict is that it calls for equalization of investment per pupil throughout the state. Undoubtedly the well-to-do would not be enthusiastic about such an arrangement which with the same total tax burden would reduce the amount spent on their children and shift tax money to poorer districts. Localities would also complain if taxes collected were not left to their discretion for spending.

But most important, such a plan would involve simple income redistribution with the new money received by the gainers channeled into education. Capital market imperfections, which now prevent the poor from investing more in their education, could be removed by a loan program that at least in theory could allow for equalization of educational investment. Further income redistribution may be desirable, but it is certainly debatable whether the educational system is the best means of achieving this goal.

[2]Mark Blaug, *An Introduction to the Economics of Education,* Penguin, 1970, summarizes a number of studies which show that learning, measured by test scores, is more dependent on factors external to schooling such as family income, social background, and neighborhoods than on education-cost factors such as class size, faculty-student ratio, textbook expenses, etc.

Apart from the property tax controversy, an important current issue deals with the basic equity and efficiency of the public school system itself. Recently attacks have been made on the system, with substitute plans for expansion of the private sector in early schooling being advanced.

THE VOUCHER PLAN

Inequities in the Present System

To enter the current controversy over plans to widen choice in early education, and narrow the scope of government activity in this area, a good beginning toward understanding of the issues involved acknowledges that the present system of school financing contains inequities against childless families and middle-class families who send their children to private schools. The rich pay more than their share, too, but we won't worry about them. A very simplified model of public school financing, which does not deviate seriously from the actual situation in structure—if it does in dollar values used—has the wealthy and the childless subsidizing the poor with the middle class just about covering its public education costs with the taxes it pays.

To show the restriction to middle-class options on schooling and the unfair tax burden placed on the childless, let us assume a community, or school district, with five family types—one poor (P), two middle class (M_1 and M_2), one childless (N), and one rich (R). All families have one child except the poor which has three. Consider further that each symbol stands not for one family but, to get the macroeconomic or community effects, for a large group of the same number one- and three-child families.

Assume further a public school cost of $800 per child, with the P group paying nothing in taxes: M_1, M_2 $800; the N group, assumed to be of middle-class income, also paying $800; and the R group $1,600. But the last group sends its children to private schools. That is, they grumble, but they pay their school taxes out of duty, and pay in addition at least as much for the benefits of a private education out of interest.

Thus, tax income and school expenditures for the public school system have the following pattern:

Public school financing, Model 1

	P	M_1	M_2	N	R	Total	Cost per child	Expenditure per child
Tax payments	...	$800	$800	$800	$1,600	$4,000	$800	
School expenditures	$2,400	$800	$800	....	......	$4,000	....	$800

If R sent their children to the public schools, then the total cost would rise by $800, neglecting effects of the scale on operating costs. R, of course, would pay less in total for schooling, as his private school costs were eliminated. But what is more important, taxes for the middle class would rise according to this simple model. Keeping the ratio the same, R would pay $320 more and M_1, M_2, and N $160 more apiece.

Expressing the present situation in a different way, public education is as good as it is for the amount of taxes paid, assuming expense per pupil is a measure of quality, because some parents, many wealthy ones, and all childless families pay school taxes but do not have children in the public schools, If the rich sent their children to the public schools, the total taxes would have to rise to reach the same expenditure per pupil level.

That the rich contribute a great deal to the schooling of the poor, because of their high property tax, may not disturb anyone's sense of equity; they could avail themselves of the public school system and reduce their education costs considerably. But our financing system has the childless middle class paying as much in school taxes as those of the same means with children in the public schools. According to the model, they are helping to pay for the education of the poor, while the middle class with children in public schools do not. Certainly they get positive "neighborhood effects"—the social benefits of a (partially) educated citizenry from the education of the poor—but so do M_1 and M_2 who do not pay a cent for these benefits.

So much for the extra burden on the childless. Now we examine the inequity toward those middle-class families who send their children to private schools. Again, we are really not considering the transfer of one child from a public to a private school, but the total effect of a mass movement of M_2 out of the system.

Now, once more abstracting from scale effects of having fewer students to educate, total public school costs will fall by $800 as M_2 leaves and per pupil costs remain the same.

The revised model, assuming constant tax rates, becomes:

Public school financing, Model 2 (M_2 in private schools)

	P	M_1	M_2	N	R	Total	Cost per child	Expenditure per child
Tax payments	...	$640	$640	$640	$1,280	$3,200	$800	
School expenditures	$2,400	$800	....	....	......	$3,200	....	$800

Since M_2 is out of the system but still paying taxes into it, everyone's taxes can be reduced. The inequity for M_2 is clear. According to the model, M_2 is not only financing part of the education of the poor but also contributing to the education of M_1 children.

An inequity remains even if we take an unrealistic extreme position favoring public over private schools to the extent that we consider there are substantial neighborhood effects from the former and none at all from the latter. Certainly M_2 should then pay for some of the social benefits resulting from M_1's public school education. But M_1 should pay just as much for the social returns from their own education. The inequity comes from the fact that M_2 also pays for part of M_1's schooling that results in private returns enjoyed by these children. This payment, in effect, becomes a penalty for leaving the school system. M_2 pays the same tax as its economic peer group, M_1, with much less returns for its payment.

The childless families still pay more than their share for neighborhood effects. An equitable distribution of public school financing would have both M_2 and N paying some school tax, but less than M_1. Such a revision would, of course, raise taxes for M_1 and possibly for R too, the group that knows that whenever a financial change is made for the cause of equity it will be called on to pay more.

The foregoing does more than explain the inequities in the present system. It shows the dependence of the public school system on funding by nonparticipants and sets financial limits to alternative plans for educational use of the same amount of school taxes collected.

Mechanics of the Voucher Plan

Voucher plans, admittedly designed to widen the opportunities for private education, could be grafted on to the current system. The idea of issuing parents vouchers for a certain dollar value of education is attributed to Milton Friedman.[3] Later on, we will examine the pros and cons of the system, but it seems in order to discuss its mechanics of financing first.

Under the simplest plan, each parent would receive a voucher per child equal to the average cost of educating a pupil in the public school system. The parent could, if he chose, keep his child in the public school or transfer him to a private school, perhaps adding additional money to cover the higher fees of the latter.

Here we are only discussing the mechanics of a feasible voucher program, leaving for later the issue of the intrinsic merit of a healthy public system. Furthermore, we must assume that the government gives out in vouchers no more in total than it collects in school taxes; for if we are to propose a voucher system that would use more money, we would not make a valid comparison between it and the current one, which would certainly improve from an infusion of extra funds. Allowing for extra public funds under the voucher plan would not be a fair way to play the game in competing for society's favor. Success for the voucher plan that related to extra public funding would not reflect intrinsic superiority in the plan. Within this restricted framework of equal funding, the simple voucher plan simply could not be applied.

---

[3]Milton Friedman, *Capitalism and Freedom*, University of Chicago Press, 1962, chap. 6 contains his consolidation of earlier thoughts on the subject.

Since public school pupil costs are currently partly met by the taxes of those rich and middle-class families whose children are not in the public system, there would be an excess of outpayments over tax income. This program would violate the condition of keeping public education costs within revenues.

An easy way out of this dilemma would involve a sliding scale for vouchers inversely related to income. Perhaps the very wealthy would receive no voucher at all, on down to the poorest who would receive the full $800–the assumed average cost per pupil. Those who wished to could add to their voucher for more expensive private schooling. The main tangible benefit of the voucher program would be that it would lead to more spending on education, but from private not government funds, as many families supplemented their voucher with extra money for education. The present system prevents parents from spending a little more on their children's education than funded by the public schools. Consequently, they must either accept the public standards or make the larger financial leap to a tax plus private-school-fee education budget.

But there is one serious flaw to this modified voucher plan. It is financially feasible, but there would be a tendency for the gap in quality of schooling between the poor and the rest of the school population to widen. Poor children would not be able to add anything to their $800 voucher, while every other family would be in a position to increase educational expenses incrementally as it added varying amounts up to the high levels required by our most expensive private schools.

At least three suggestions have been made to correct for this glaring shortcoming of the modified voucher plan. Far be it from the wishes of its adherents to propose a program that would put more weight on the heavy side of our already unbalanced socioeconomic scale.

First, there is the idea of increasing the size of the voucher for the poor beyond the $800 level. This suggestion can be rejected out of hand as not playing the present system-voucher plan comparison game fairly. To give those who are paying nothing, or even those who are paying less in taxes than their education costs, more than the average school costs would redistribute education expenditures to the poor and would require a rise in school costs for the others to maintain the same level of educational investment in their own children. Supporters of the present system could also argue that compensatory education–

what this plan amounts to—financed by additional taxes might work wonders in improving the current system. If the voucher system is to be compared with the current system, then it would be unfair to cite advantages on the basis of more available funding. Expressed differently, a voucher system that included compensatory spending—extra resources applied to overcome the disadvantages of poverty or discrimination or both—would have to be compared with a public system that also received extra money for this needed purpose. This comparison could be made. It is worth noting, though, that compensatory education is an absolute requirement of this adjustment to the voucher system to keep it from exacerbating quality differences in education between poor and nonpoor because of the feature of the system that encouraged extra private educational spending by the latter.

The second suggestion, to correct for a tendency toward growing disparity in educational quality, places strict limitations on private school fees by forcing all such schools to accept the voucher as full payment for tuition. This means that these schools could collect only $800 per student.

This plan would help maintain the current distribution of educational quality, outside of existing private schools, but would eliminate the one tangible advantage of the voucher system—the encouragement of higher family spending on schooling. Further it would have a drastic effect on existing private schools. They would be prevented from offering all the services they now provide if their income were cut by the requirement that they accept vouchers as full tuition payment.

The third plan would not allow vouchers to be used for schools that charged more than the value of the voucher. That is, vouchers could not be received by schools that charged (additional) tuition.

This plan allows parents to choose to continue sending their children to private schools, at the same time double cost of taxes and fees. But again, this voucher system would not encourage additional private spending on education. Parents could only use vouchers to send their children to inexpensive private schools—those budgeted at a per pupil outlay equal to or less than that of the public schools.

A "Model Voucher System"

This plan to limit the use of vouchers to schools that accept them as full instructional payment forms the core of an Office of Economic

Opportunity's (OEO) voucher experimental program. What the OEO calls a model voucher system contains other features and safeguards as well.[4]

To avoid the temptation for the new schools that arose from the infusion of voucher funds to select the better students—the ones that will make their "production" record look good—the model system requires the schools to accept all those who apply. If the school had more applications than places, it would have to fill half its acceptances by lot.

Then, there is an important provision to prevent racial discrimination in school admission policy. Each school would have to accept at least as high a percentage of minority students as have applied. In addition, transportation costs would be provided for those students who choose schools outside their neighborhoods. (There is also mention of larger vouchers for poorer students, but we still reject this as an invalid component of a program that purports to offer, *by its nature,* better education than the present system. Anyway, the admission requirements, if followed, should provide for adequate coverage of the poor and of racial minorities.)

Demonstrating an uninhibited amount of bad logic, defenders of this proposal argue that it will lead to greater school integration as it broke down the "neighborhood school" pattern of the current public system which fosters school segregation in line with housing segregation. There is no defense for the current system that permits school districts and even whole communities, usually suburban ones, to isolate themselves from what they consider the corroding influence of interracial instruction.

But by what reasoning or reference to experience would we expect better from a full-blown private system? The story of Civil Rights legislation in the United States has been one of earlier compliance with the law by the government or public sector with private organizations lagging behind, whether employers, clubs, or sellers of goods and services. In education, no one has ever accused private schools of being hotbeds of movements for social reform. The thought that integration would be fostered under (federal) government regulations that enforced

---

[4]*Education Vouchers,* Preliminary Report, Center for the Study of Public Policy, 1970. For a brief summary of the report, see Christopher Jencks, "Education Vouchers," *The New Republic,* July 1970.

freedom of choice for all to attend the many private schools that would spring up and that provided free transportation to students who wanted to go to these institutions implies that the government would have more success in desegregating reluctant private schools than it has had in local government-run systems, and/or that blacks would be welcome if they came in small busses.

It is true that courts have more success in desegregating private units than public ones which ostensibly do not discriminate. But those with strong racist sentiments would know what they would be getting into if they accepted this strictly directed program and would fight against it no less than they do against integration of the public schools today. Adherents of the voucher system point out that the bigot does not need a(n) (unregulated) voucher system to practice schooling segregation; he is having great success within the public system. But the shoe is really on the other foot. The voucher advocate must explain why his substitute-regulated system which guaranteed greater desegregation would gain wider acceptance among adherents of the status quo.

No wonder that both the bigot and the fair-minded can, in principle, support a voucher system. The former sees it as a way of institutionalizing segregation; the latter as a means to introduce integration by special provisions. The ensuing battle royal would be no less contentious than the current bitter struggle over busing and other reforms to alter racial patterns within the present system.

Within the present public system, elimination of the property tax basis would do much to reduce suburban isolation by removing the incentive of better, that is, more highly budgeted public schools. In any case, the best hope for greater interracial harmony, if it really can be achieved through broadened contacts at early ages, is through reform of the public schools, not substitution of a system that is inherently separatist. One is reminded of the poet's good advice to the pale maiden—"If looking well won't win him, will looking ill prevail?"

In summary, to retain the one tangible advantage of the voucher system of greater private spending on education[5] and at the same time

[5]We can assume that economies resulting from private competition in education would be offset by the diseconomies arising from the large number of small schools that might appear with implementation of the voucher system. We have not even mentioned the danger of hucksterism that might mislead the unwary under the expanded private system of education management. The OEO plan hopes that supervision of advertising and requirement of full disclosures of programs and policies by individual schools will minimize this danger.

not to widen the relative disadvantage of the poor requires provision of higher tax payments, which would undoubtedly benefit the existing system, or strict government regulation of private school financial and admission policies, or both. Apart from the gain of increased spending on schooling, proponents of voucher plans also note the advantage of greater choice in schooling they offer parents. We now turn to that argument.

Choice and the Voucher System

If one cites the advantage of choice that a fully developed private system will provide, he must obviously imply not only that private schools will differ as a whole from the public system but also that there must be significant differences among the individual schools. But how will they differ? What with national testing results playing so important a part in the admission standards of our colleges, especially the more prestigious ones, they will not differ much in the direction, if perhaps they do in the quality of their instruction.

Thus, they must differ in other areas—in their social or religious orientation and perhaps in their political leanings. The result will be a greater compartmentalization of viewpoints—if first among parents—to be developed at school among children. Friedman himself raises the spirit of divisiveness that might be nurtured through the proliferation of private schools but discounts the danger by citing that the public school system inhibits individual freedom of thought and belief.

Minimizing a shortcoming by admitting it is so is an old rhetorical dodge. Cicero was an expert at this type of argument: "So my client is a charlatan, wife-beater, and embezzler—but let's look at the important facets of his character." One need not be an alarmist about the dangers of social divisiveness that might arise from an expanded private system. As long as competition for college places remains strong, schools will satisfy family wants by spending more energy and resources in providing an education that will result in high SAT scores than in conformity to religious, social, or political orthodoxy.

Expansion of private schools, though, would result in more social separation than we now have. If public schools have been guilty of indoctrination in what might be accepted as wholesome values consistent with our stated national philosophy—of understanding, brotherhood, and human equality—they have undeniably done a miserable job. But can we solve our social ills by withdrawing into our own narrow spheres of interest?

Friedman claims that under voucher plans the government's intervention in school administration would be simply to set minimum standards of program contents and that its supervisory role would be similar to its inspection of restaurants to assure conformity with sanitary requirements. We have seen that the state would have to do much more, in effect substituting broader bureaucratic control over admission policy and financing compared with what it now exercises over the public system.

In any case, man is not a machine, but neither is education an egg salad sandwich. Rather than the give-and-take of conflicting views that forge local goals of our public schools, the expansion in the private system that would follow implementation of voucher plans would lead to a growth in institutions, each with its own narrow orientation unmodified by the need to adjust to different viewpoints. Unlike restaurants, where the quality of food once it passes minimum health standards would have no lasting effects, education will condition the child toward his lifetime attitudes. In schools which offer a choice among doctrines as well as quality of formal instruction, it is doubtful whether the child will experience much ideological conflict or even need to develop an understanding of the other views on social issues he will face in later life. Instead of thirty-one different flavors of education, the voucher system may well create thirty-one narrow centers for the pursuit of self-interest. While we want diversity, we may get division.

Supporters of the voucher system ask champions of the public schools why they do not argue for the elimination of all private schools. Why should the rich be privileged to engage in antisocial behavior, by sending their children to private schools? This would indeed be an extreme position. It is one thing to say that society benefits from strong public schools and another to say that sending children to private schools constitutes an antisocial act. Certainly free elections and the maintenance of democracy require many voters. But we do not make voting mandatory. It might be made so if the percentage eligible who voted shrank to such low levels as to threaten the principles of democratic choice. But no defender of the public school system claims that today's private schools pose a threat to our society.

If some families wish to indulge their tastes for private education by meeting today's high costs, they should be free to do so. This is a far different view from advocating a plan that would make private schools the dominant form of early educational institution.

To close on a note of compromise, if equitable financial reforms are made in the public system, the development of private schools will be encouraged anyway. The end of the property tax would make many high-valued property owners disenchanted with the public system; what is the need for a private school if your child can attend a high-income enclave's "public" school which spends $1,500 per pupil per year? A statewide equal-cost educational system would drive many of these parents to the private schools. In a less negative way, the reform suggested above of reducing tax payments of those parents who send their children to private schools below the level paid by those living in housing of the same value whose children attend public schools would surely provide a fillip to private school growth.

SUMMARY

The present system of public school financing, based on the property tax, is under attack. Certainly those pupils living in high-income, more exactly, high-cost housing neighborhoods have a greater amount invested in their schooling than children of poorer districts. Defenders of the status quo argue that the rich have greater spending power over all goods, so why not in education, too. As long as minimum standards are set, as they are in health and other areas of "fundamental interest" to each citizen, then–the argument continues–the more affluent should be able to enjoy more expensive schooling.

The rebuttal to this view holds that capital market imperfections prevent the poor from obtaining quality (high-cost) schooling through loans. The result is that high-income children enjoy high rates of return on their schooling, based on monopoly elements which allow expensive schooling only to those who can finance it out of their own resources.

The California decision which bans the property tax as a basis for school financing says nothing about a substitute plan. But the presumption is that there should be a move toward equalization of per pupil costs across the state. If no more school taxes are collected in total, this change would redistribute income. It is debatable whether further redistribution, if desirable, should be carried out through the operation of the school system.

There are other inequities in our current system besides the handicaps in getting good schooling faced by the poor. Childless families and middle-class families who send their children to private schools pay more than their share for society's positive "neighborhood effects," received from the education of the poor. Expressed differently, the public schools can spend as much as they do per pupil in the system because many families pay school taxes who have no children in the system.

To compare the merits of a voucher plan with the current system should require that such a plan does not use more tax funds than are currently employed within the existing public system.

Thus, each one-child family cannot receive a voucher equal to the average cost per child in the system. A sliding scale could be developed whereby vouchers would be distributed with differential values up to the total of current taxes collected. A larger voucher could not be given to poorer than to middle-class children, though, if we wanted to compare the voucher plan with the current system, because this would represent *compensatory education,* which could be included in the current public system.

To prevent schools from selecting only the better students and from practicing racial discrimination tight admission rules could be established. But, then, it is doubtful whether the regulated voucher plan would gain any more adherents than a liberalized public school system would. The provision designed to avoid preference for higher-income applicants that required voucher-supported schools to accept the voucher as full-fee payment would remove one of the most attractive features of the program—the increase in private spending on education.

Vouchers would widen the choice among schools. But there is serious question whether this proliferation of schools, which would undeniably weaken our current public school system, would lead to diversity or division.

CHAPTER EIGHT

Financing College Education

The social benefits of education related to the advantages in maintaining a democratic society by having an informed electorate tend to decline as the level of education rises. Our way of political life is not threatened because we do not all have graduate degrees. It is a safe assumption that these social gains are less from college than from high school education.

But while some social benefits might wane in importance, the private nonmonetary benefits intensify from high school graduation through college. We are fast making the college degree the *sine qua non* for all important positions of responsibility and power. On the other side of the coin, those whose schooling terminates at high school are practically precluded from leadership in most areas of society. The strongest position regarding the value of college would make it of "fundamental interest" to the individual, implying that everyone who wants one should receive a college education, which is a far distance from the view that everyone who can benefit from it should go to college—whatever that may mean—and light years away from the old-fashioned principle that there is a college for everyone who can pay for it.

Since the gains from college fall mainly to the student, in later life, considerable social benefits notwithstanding, there are many who conclude that he should therefore pay for it. If everyone could pay for his college education out of his own or family's resources, there would be no financing problem. Some might reject the opportunity for this education because of lack of interest or motivation, but society would feel no guilt or shame at not serving its members. On the other hand, if college is held a "fundamental interest," or less strongly and without the element of necessity that term contains—society considers that the opportunity for college should be available to all—then the question of financing policy becomes important since many potential students cannot now finance their college expenses.

Thus, college-financing policy refers to the means adopted for satisfying society's goal for expanded opportunity for higher education of its members. College is expensive. Direct costs to cover instructional salaries, buildings, equipment, etc., are high and indirect costs of foregone earnings for eighteen- to twenty-two-year-olds much above those for the years of earlier schooling. There is no exaggeration in estimating current total costs at $40,000 for the four years. Not many individuals can cover the costs themselves. State and local universities use tax funds to meet part of the costs for their students, but contrary to popular belief this aid does not cover a very large share of the costs. Almost all tax-financed institutions require some fee payments for their students, and they only seldom cut into the largest segment of costs—foregone earnings. Scholarships and fellowships also help. But we have no systematic national plan for funding the education of the bulk of the population for whom raising $40,000 over four years would, to put it mildly, represent an economic hardship.

But the issue of college-financing policy centers about a lower figure than actual costs. While costs, as discussed in Chapter 2, including foregone earnings—because they represent an important investment input—serve as the basis of economic decision making on college investment, financing refers to the means of meeting these costs. Expressed in accounting terms, costs are expenses, while financing for actual outlays refers to expenditures.

Thus the student who must just cover his direct cost and maintenance expenses requires less financing than the dollar value of costs. This does not deny that he should use the cost figure, not the financing one, in evaluating the profitability of college. The same should be done by public authorities in their social decisions. If four years of college cost $40,000, it seems realistic to assume $20,000 will cover financing needs for the typical student.

Despite these high costs, empirical studies conclude that the direct monetary returns, not counting indirect nonmonetary and social benefits, exceed costs by at least enough to yield a normal return. But since the calculated values are of average yields, and recalling the analysis of Chapter 6 which held that marginal rates are somewhat lower than average rates, the discussion in this chapter will consider that the marginal rate for the further investment that easier financing would allow, on average, matches the (opportunity cost) rate on alternative investment of the same risk and liquidity.

Society has at least two other compelling reasons for seeking ways to facilitate college financing besides serving individuals' "fundamental interest" and gaining the added social benefits of a more educated citizenry. Even if the *"average"* marginal rate of return were close to or at its equilibrium (alternative) rate, there would still be opportunities for improving the efficiency of total investment by reaching out to aid those insolvent students whose education would yield high returns if they could only meet their current school expenses. National output would increase by directing investment funds to these students.

Of course, no one knows the exact count of academically able students whose schooling is foreclosed by financial or social background handicaps, but circumstantial evidence indicates that their number is not insignificant. A leading new text in summarizing studies on college attainment by socioeconomic and ability classes notes that while in 1966 among the most able category 95 percent classified in the high socioeconomic group based on family income, father's educational attainment, and other factors attended college, only 50 percent in the low socioeconomic group went. Of those in the bottom quintile of ability, 40 percent of the high and only 15 percent of the low socioeconomic group attended.[1] Considering family income alone, the same text reports that in 1966 only 14 percent of all families but 41 percent of college student families had incomes over $10,000. At the lower end of the scale, 14 percent of all families and only 4 percent of college families had incomes below $3,000. Income deficiency is a serious handicap for blacks, going a long way to explain their low college attendance. The median parental income of white college students was about $10,000 and only $5,000 for blacks.

[1]Sar Levitan, Garth Mangum, and Ray Marshall, *Human Resources and Labor Markets,* Harper & Row, 1972.

The second reason for national concern over college financing relates to the problem of poverty. There is strong correlation between low earnings and little schooling. Education is looked upon as an excellent self-help device in raising incomes of the poor. With schooling and training they will become qualified for good-paying jobs and lift themselves out of poverty.

There is no disputing this argument, as far as it goes. Certainly there is a vicious circle of poverty and low education. The latter almost assures low-paying jobs, if any, and incomes so low are unable to finance more schooling. Financial aid for college education would contribute a good deal to breaking the circle, but so would $20,000 directed to many other investments in behalf of each poor individual.

Looking farther into the issue just raised, Adam Smith's description of labor earnings and income in a perfectly competitive world gives us some insights into the question of eliminating poverty through education. As Smith explained, under perfectly competitive labor market conditions—full opportunity for freedom of occupational choice, perfect knowledge, and purely economic motivation—we would all earn the same wage. (Smith does allow for some compensating factors in lieu of wages, such as pleasant work and employment security.) Differences in earnings, though, would arise which, while they appeared in wages, really represented returns to investment in education and training.

No one doubts that the American labor market is anything but perfectly competitive. Nevertheless, a great deal of the differences in income in the United States can be explained by differences in the level of education among workers, so that a large part of higher wages does not truly represent greater pay for labor contribution, but returns to earlier investment. In countries where physical capital dominates investment, the link between incomes and returns to capital becomes clearer, since these returns do not appear in the wage payment, but in rent, interest, and dividend income. Correction of wages to separate returns to human capital would make the imbalance in our (labor) earnings much less pronounced, even if this adjustment did not affect our income distribution.

Thus, a basic reason for poverty which continues even with full-time work and labor income is more a shortage of capital than a lack of education. Proposals to finance the education of the poor as a means to reduce poverty are then really designed to provide them with this capital—grants—or give them access to and the use of capital—loans. In either case, the overall effect will be to raise the later income of the poor who receive education—this income—to the extent labor market competition prevails, in the form of returns to the educational investment they receive.

EDUCATION LOANS VERSUS GRANTS IN REDUCING POVERTY

You do not have to be poor to be unable to raise $20,000, the assumed financing needs for a college education. But it helps in concentrating on the two goals of public policy—to improve investment efficiency by funding those whose rate of return on college investment would exceed average returns and to reduce poverty—into one by comparing the effects of loan-and-grant policy with reference to the poor as recipients.

Those with inadequate educational investment funds face capital market imperfections in borrowing. These imperfections either keep them from borrowing at all or allow them to borrow only at rates above the level on alternative investments. Loans to college students would be at high rates anyway in the absence of repayment guarantees to the lenders because of their previously discussed risk and illiquidity.

Recall that in Chapter 2's discussion of financing costs for borrowing students, the appropriate discount rate, or alternative rate, for comparison with the internal rate of return was not some average rate for investment similar in risk and illiquidity to schooling but to the actual borrowing rate if it were higher. Thus, many would-be college students are deterred from education by the high interest costs which make an otherwise profitable investment economically unsound. To use a numerical example, if a student could earn 12 percent on a college investment but must pay a loan rate of 15 percent college would not "pay" for him, in what we have become accustomed to call the crude direct economic sense of the word. That the rate was 10 percent for loans of similar risk and illiquidity has no effect on the negative economic influence of the investment decision of a high loan rate.[2]

[2]This, of course, assumes he borrows to cover all his costs. In the above example, if he borrows to meet half his costs, his effective opportunity cost rate is 12½ percent, that is, ½ (15% + 10%), which is still higher than 12 percent. Obviously, the less money borrowed, the more likely college would "pay" for him.

It would, though, influence public decision on financing education. If a rate made high because of capital market imperfections discouraged investment whose returns exceeded their opportunity costs, then total output could be increased by measures to remove these imperfections. In what follows, loan policy will refer to the efforts to provide education loans at competitive rates, those on alternative investments of similar risk and liquidity. Any lower rate charged would in effect give the borrowers a form of subsidy and would be closer in kind to a grant than to what can be called a market loan, a loan at competitive interest rates.

To begin with a special case, suppose a loan program of government guarantees permits a poor individual to borrow at the assumed 10 percent market rate. Consider the effect of the loan in lifting him out of poverty, if he realizes a 10 percent return on his investment. Under these conditions his earnings would rise, but his poverty would remain unaffected by his higher gross income. After payment of his annual amortization and interest charges, he would be left with the same income he would have earned had he not gone to college.

Think of the calamitous social effects if such a result were general. Aid to education as a means of eliminating poverty would be a lifetime delusion for the poor. All their income gains after four years of advanced schooling would go to satisfy lenders, backed by, if not actually a part of, the government, who demanded repayment through the borrower's work life. Society is used to long-term loans, but would it tolerate a system of repayments so closely tied to the borrower's earnings, obligations which drive the payers back into permanent poverty? Would the poor and the many who sympathized with their plight be comforted by the logic that those who financed their own schooling, which yielded the same gross returns, enjoyed a much higher standard of living not because of economic inequity or discrimination against the poor but simply because they started with more capital which was only earning them normal returns invested in education?

Obviously, a loan program of this type would break down. If repayment were made, nothing would have been done to reduce poverty. More likely, pressures would arise from all sides to make collection on these loans difficult if not impossible.

No mention has been made of residual consumption benefits for the educated poor. In fact these benefits might actually be negative. Since wealth carries its own importance, it is doubtful whether responsible positions in society outside the market place would be attained as a result of schooling when the educated people in question lived under poverty conditions. Knowledge and culture, the fruits of a good college education, would be sour grapes to those who could not afford to enjoy them. Stated simply, without belaboring the point further, a market-loan program which financed the education of those poor who could realize only normal returns on the investment just would not work; it would not serve its purpose of reducing poverty.

But what of a loan program to finance the college education of those who have been unfortunately called the able poor—as if the general words capacity and ineptitude referred solely to one's potential college performance—those who could earn more than the normal rate on their college investment? Now, if the student earned 12 percent and borrowed at 10 percent—the rate to which college loans would be lowered by the government financed program—he would have a net income gain from college, even after repayment of his annual amortization and interest charges.

At first view it appears that a loan program for these students would be helpful and feasible. But the gains are small indeed. Making a very rough calculation and ignoring complications of discounting, with an investment of $40,000 for college, a net return after payment of loan costs of 2 percent would add about $800 to average annual earnings, including, of course, the four years from 18 to 22 of negative returns of foregone earnings.[3] This amount would do very little to alleviate poverty. Estimating net returns at about $400 per year for every percentage point of rate of return above 10 percent would require an internal rate of perhaps 20 percent to give the poor a significant push toward middle-class status. Very few individuals, poor or otherwise, have such cheery prospects of economic returns on their college investment.

It might be argued that rates of return are much higher for poor students because their foregone earnings both as students and in later life would be much below average. But to counter this favorable influence on the rate of return, the typically weak early education of the poor reduces the effectiveness of a given amount of college investment

---

[3]Since the loan rate is assumed equal to the average rate of return, the net-earnings calculation is not affected if only part of costs are financed by borrowing.

in improving their academic skills and, presumably, their later earning power. Therefore, we can still conclude that college loans to the poor would lead only a very few out of poverty and would make an ineffective national program to raise the general economic level of our lowest income group.

This leads us back to the earlier conclusion that incomes are low for those who lack capital, but the above discussion of the inadequacy of a loan program to raise net income points out that what would help the poor toward higher net incomes is not the use of capital, but its possession. This shortage could be filled by a grant program, and to be effective, grants would have to be expanded to cover the considerable maintenance costs, not just direct school costs.

The possibilities of improving the economic status and social and emotional well-being of the poor through an extensive grant program are enormous. If the program is well run to include remedial and compensatory instruction to compensate for the slow start toward college learning the typical poor eighteen-year-old has received before college entrance, returns from this schooling should be high. In fact, private rates of return of infinity is almost a can't-miss prediction for grantees. With zero costs, any earnings above what could have been earned without college training would lead to this happy result. More realistically, if grants finance one-half of the total college costs, the student could net as little as 60 percent of these costs to make college "pay."

The social implications from a grant program require closer examination and raise some questions. Grants must be financed by taxpayers, and if the program is large enough, it will involve a giant transfer of income from taxpayers to human investment in the poor. On the surface there seems nothing wrong with this practice. There are already many transfer programs, and what better one could be designed than one to improve the earning power of the poor so that they can rise above poverty through their own efforts rather than through the constant transfer of funds to maintain a low consumption standard.

But questions of efficiency in the use of public funds, and the interests of the poor themselves, arise. As to the first, admittedly there is an appeal in a self-help program initiated by a prior burst of investment funds, which slow and steady consumption support funds do not have. But if rates of return on investment are below market levels on the educational investment, then to achieve the same amount of poverty reduction the cost to the government of the grant program would be higher than that of a simple income supplement plan.

A basis for selection would have to be established. With provision not only of direct school expenses but maintenance costs as well, applicants would probably include many whose chances of a social rate of return as high as 10 percent were very slim. If grants were made available only to those who showed promise of yielding such a high rate, given the prior educational disadvantages of the average poor eighteen-year-old, to say nothing of restricted opportunities for better jobs later even to those who learn well, the program would be quickly recognized as another perhaps well-intentioned but practically ineffective anti-poverty device.

Certainly, the public decision makers would have to reach down to those who indicated a below-10 percent rate-of-return potential. Such a practice could not entirely be charged against investment efficiency because of the considerable social gains that would accrue from the work-related and other consumption benefits from education that would be enjoyed by the grantees. Then there would be the gains to society as a whole, both from a more highly educated citizenry and the psychological as well as monetary uplift to the former poor.

But still some selection would have to be made, some cutoff point established, based somewhat on earnings potential. The state would have to keep in mind differential consumption benefits from different academic pursuits so as not to be trapped into a program that financed only those forms of schooling which promised the highest monetary returns—science and professions over liberal arts, vocationally oriented curricula over academically oriented curricula. The basis of selection would be further complicated by the difficulty of predicting school success—much less future earning power—for a group largely handicapped by inferior early schooling.

As for the poor themselves, the presumption is that those who did not qualify for educational grants, by whatever standards are finally set, would continue to receive income supplements. There is nothing new in federal subsidies to special groups, but if the government truly wishes to alleviate economic misery through investment rather than through consumption support, it should broaden the program to provide physical capital as well as human capital funds. Many among the poor who might not show academic promise or interest could realize high returns from physical capital investment. Specifically, business and commercial grants, not loans, could be made to parallel human capital investments in "the more able"—and how arrogant is that designation to refer to those who would make better use of human capital compared to those who might earn high business returns. These added grants should be made in the cause of efficiency as well as equity.

Obviously, investment programs in the poor would be costly, especially if as is maintained above, the only practical financing program to push hard against poverty through expanded higher education would entail grants and not loans. But those who think any meaningful antipoverty measures would be cheap are deluding the poor, and themselves, or perhaps others for the noble end, if not means, of gaining political acceptance of worthwhile programs.

If loan financing cannot be used effectively on a large scale for the college education of the poor, it still has considerable value in aiding the nonpoor, many who find $40,000 or even $20,000 too much to raise out-of-pocket or by reduced consumption and part-time work or through conventional bank loans. In any case, the American public (voters), though perfectly willing to support affluent business and agriculture on occasion, is not conditioned to outright gifts of public funds to individuals not in need.

COLLEGE LOAN AND EQUITY INVESTMENT PROGRAMS

Since the estimated marginal rate of return on college investment about equals that on alternative investments, it would appear that a government loan program could be self-financing, with market rates earned by the government agency as it provided the helpful service of removing imperfections in the capital market. But since loans are made at fixed rates, while rates of return on education vary widely among individuals, even though the average rate might exceed market rates on similar loans, the financial structure of the program would soon collapse. At an established rate of say, 10 percent, some could make repayment easily, but others not so fortunate or capable in translating learning into higher earnings could not repay their loans, if they could do so at all, except at the cost of reducing their incomes to levels below what they would have been had they not gone to college. This situation, of course, arises only for cases in which the loans finance all or at least a large part of the individual's college investment.

The sight of the government dunning economically unsuccessful graduates for repayment of ill-advised loans would be socially intolerable. Even if in many cases principal and interest could be recouped, losses by default would arise so that for the program to avoid losses would require an interest rate above the assumed market level of 10 percent. This adjustment would defeat the whole purpose of the program, which is to correct for market imperfections that make financing of college education so high for the insolvent. If losses were expected and funded from taxes, then we would be speaking of a modified grant rather than a loan program.

What is obviously needed is a program that would allow for variations in repayment terms to take into account the vast differences in individual returns realized. A simple way suggested by many analysts of the problem to achieve this end is through a system of equity financing in which the recipient would pay into the fund an annual amount, determined by the level of his future earnings.[4] The investment would have loan features too in that annual repayments on average would have to cover the principal because of the limited work life span of the recipient. Inasmuch as average rates of return on college investment are high enough to permit average returns to the fund at market rates, a schedule of "profit distribution"—as these payments by financed graduates would technically be—in line with earnings could be devised to make the entire program self-financing. This equity type of financing would have the additional advantage of not placing the government in the embarrassing if not socially unacceptable position of pressing for repayment from those who could least afford it. Those who profited less from college investment would be required to pay out less in dividends.

But since the average rate of return on college investment is not much more than market rates on alternative similar investments, it

[4]Such proposals are made by Milton Friedman, *Capitalism and Freedom,* Office of Education, 1962; William Vickrey, "A Proposal for Student Loans," in Selma Mushkin (ed.), *Economics of Higher Education.* There is also a government study group recommendation for an Educational Opportunity Bank. James Tobin and Leonard Ross, "A National Youth Endowment," *New Republic,* vol. 160, May 3, 1969, urge that such a program be extended to cover vocational training and education as well as college costs.

might seem that there would be little gain to the borrowers in a self-financing equity program of this type. Those who earned more after college would pay higher dividends, but if all financed their entire investment through the program, each would have to pay out more or less the same amount as he received in extra earnings from college.

This dreary result, though, only applies to those who finance all or almost all their schooling through the loan-equity program. In effect, we have just repeated the shortcoming of a loan program for the poor, who would be the ones in this position.[5] For those who could finance a substantial part of their college investment through their own resources or efforts, repayment at market rates would not push their net income down much, even if the required dividend rate about matched their returns on educational investment. They would retain all the returns from investment of their own funds.

In fact, the great benefits of any financing program lies in its provision of marginal funds to facilitate the attainment of a college education. Investment in college requires a great deal of money, but what matters here is that to be an effective source of higher future earning power the investment must be total. Within limits, physical capital investments may be in varying amounts, without undue effects on earning rates; but such gradations in investment are not feasible for college. All rate-of-return studies show a drastically lower rate for partial investment compared to that of the complete four-year program. These rates characteristically fall below the comparative rate on alternative investments. Thus, if a student could not finance his whole college education, he is currently deterred from undertaking any of it. Assured lending power can turn many an uneconomic decision for college investment into a profitable one.

A dichotomous financing plan whereby, following some arbitrary definition of poverty, the poor were to receive grants and the nonpoor loans would make no sense at all. Apart from the difficulties of admini-

---

[5]The Yale Plan, an early private college program for learning now, paying later with payments dependent on the level of future earnings, meets this problem by scaling payments very low, below cost, for low-income earners. For example, a $3,000 later average income will only have to pay back $155 of a $1,000 loan. Of course, those with large incomes have to pay a relatively high rate on their loans, discouraging participation of the wealthy in the program. For detailed analysis of the Yale Plan, see Robert W. Hartman, "Equity Implications of State Tuition Policy and Student Loans," *Journal of Political Economy*, vol. 80, May-June 1972.

stration such an arrangement would create, with many straining to be classified as poor for obvious monetary advantages, our sense of equity would be offended. The progressive income tax has become a way of national economic life, and we relish in taxing the rich heavily, or at least trying to. But we would not like our marginal tax rates to exceed 100 percent, or, analogously, an educational subsidy program raise net earnings for those who receive the subsidy enough to surpass those at the same gross earnings level who do not, even if we were unconcerned about disincentive effects.

A funding program, though, could be easily designed which allowed for higher net income the more the individual financed his college education from his own resources, for those earning the same rate of return on their total college investment. To follow this principle would require that no one receive a total grant because such recipients would net as much as those who financed their schooling entirely out of their own resources and more than those who borrowed any amount no matter how small. But the inability to receive a full grant would not much weaken the antipoverty impact of the program. The poorer the individual, the larger would be his grant. His loan would also be larger, in keeping with the equity principle of higher net returns to those who finance more of their own educational investment.

Table 8-1 shows how a simple grant-loan (equity) program could work. Total college costs of $40,000 require $20,000 in financing. The student who finances his entire schooling receives no grants or loans, on down to the student who contributes nothing from his own resources but borrows $10,000 and receives a $10,000 grant from a government fund. For simplicity's sake, the rate of return on total college

TABLE 8-1
A grant-loan program for financing college
(10% internal rate of return for all students)

Own money	$ ...	$4,000	$8,000	$12,000	$16,000	$20,000
Grant	10,000	8,000	6,000	4,000	2,000	
Loan	10,000	8,000	6,000	4,000	2,000	
Annual net earnings retained by student	$2,900	$3,160	$3,420	$ 3,680	$ 3,940	$ 4,200

investment is assumed to be the same, 10 percent for all. Further simplifying, assumptions are a repayment period of thirty-five years after college with constant earnings each year.

The important last row shows the amount of earnings above the average high school level retained by each student after repayment of interest and principal on his loan. Thus the student who does not borrow keeps his full $4,200 of extra annual earnings. The student who borrows $6,000, for example, pays off his loan with 10 percent interest in equal installments of $780 each year, keeping $3,420 of his extra earnings each year.

The investment is a marginal decision for the self-financing student but is a profitable one for all others because they have part of their investment subsidized by grants. But those who finance most of their own schooling end up with a higher net income.

A system that included grants as well as loans would help solve one of the major incentive problems of the modified equity program. If dividend payments are related to the size of later earnings, the program is made self-financing, and rates of return on college are not much higher than on alternative investment; then if all participants borrowed their full college costs, no one would be any better off financially because of his education. Relative to the disincentive effect, graduates would have no economic motivation to earn more because all their extra earnings would go back to the fund in dividends to compensate for the low payments of the financially less successful. But if loans finance only a part of the total investment, then the disincentive effect would be less—the weaker the smaller the amount borrowed—because only the portion borrowed would require higher dividend payments. The rest would be retained by the graduate. Even under the more realistic conditions with only part of his total costs financed, the disincentive effects are weakened if some financing is by grants.

To give a numerical example, if two students had 20 percent of their equal college costs funded by loans through the program, the first who earned a 15 percent return would keep 12 percent after paying dividends of 15 percent on the publicly funded part of his investment. The second who earned only 5 percent would retain 4 percent after repayment under this simple formula. Absolute income differentials would narrow because of the connection between earnings and repayment rates, but economic incentive to gross higher income would not be seriously affected.

As with a grant program, some fear arises that the fund's managers will favor applications of students whose course of study promises the highest average financial returns. They would be under stronger pressure to follow this practice because to be politically acceptable the lending part of the fund would probably be budgeted to be self-financing; a self-financing grant program is a contradiction in terms. But an equity program with a sliding-scale dividend formula would greatly reduce this danger of favoring financially promising curricula. Unlike the condition of fixed interest loans, the managers would be certain of breaking even, in the economic sense of earning a normal rate of return on total educational investment, as long as the average rate of return for the "borrowers" was as high as this normal rate.

On the demand side for these funds, students would no longer be discouraged by rigid loan rates from fields of below-average financial returns but which promised them high consumption benefits, at least from their viewpoint at age eighteen.

PUBLIC FINANCING OF HIGHER EDUCATION

It seems paradoxical that state universities, many established upwards of a hundred years ago, which were founded on the principle of widening opportunities for a college education to all are now less favored, and their policies criticized, when this principle is stronger than ever. It is not that the state universities are remiss in following this principle, for while some of them have become more selective over the years, their recent expansion in sheer numbers practically assures a place at some state school for every applicant. What has come under attack is their financing policies, especially their practice of providing the same subsidized low cost to all regardless of means.

While there have been recent relatively small programs to give special subsidies to poorer students, including in some instances maintenance allowances, by far the greatest part of state financed subsidies takes the form of a reduction in direct costs—tuition and fees—to all students.

As such, the current method of finance closely parallels the pattern that would evolve for the public school system if the property tax basis of funding and distribution were eliminated. Families would probably pay a graduated income tax to finance the schools, as they now do for state colleges; and the money spent per pupil would be equalized through the individual school districts, as per student costs now are for those in state college systems.

But reform in public early education finance has been suggested to strengthen acceptance of the system. Support of public higher education on the grounds that it produces social benefits that a private system cannot provide can surely be challenged. Considering their size, fixed investment, and political acceptance, there is no practical point in disputing the merits of public administration of colleges. These schools undoubtedly arose to fill a need, based greatly on the inability of private colleges to serve an expanded number of applicants—most of them with inadequate resources to cover total college expenses and many unable to fund even direct tuition costs. This inability in turn stemmed from weakness in the capital market and the absence of a comprehensive grant-loan (equity) program.

Such a program would help toward making the private colleges more competitive with the public ones—now they have in the main only private donations to compare with tax income as a source of reduction from full-cost tuition. But, at least insofar as direct costs are concerned, private colleges would still be at a disadvantage as long as state colleges provided what amounts to outright grants of reduced direct costs to their students.

What would be needed to put private and public systems on an equal footing would be a system of grants and equity investing of the type described above for both. This would require a change in state school financing, reducing grant assistance in step with financial resources of the students. But this modification seems consistent with most people's understanding of equity. Many states are currently considering the step toward reducing public subsidies to more affluent students.

Hansen and Weisbrod have suggested a plan for the state of Wisconsin which lowers college costs for poorer students and raises them, at least for state colleges and universities, for those wealthy enough to finance their schooling out of their own resources.[6] Their plan was

---

[6]W. Lee Hansen and Burton Weisbrod, "A New Approach to Higher Education Finance," in Mel Orwigg (ed.), *Financing Higher Education*, The American College Testing Program, 1971.

motivated by their earlier study of benefits and costs of the California public higher education system.[7] They found that with the state schools subsidizing all students, eligibility at the higher subsidized schools was positively related to income, and participation rates at all these schools was also related to income. Progressivity in income taxes did not compensate for the extra benefits of high-income students.

It is one thing to question whether school systems are a good agent for income redistribution, from rich to poor, as would be the case of a grant program focused on low-income students. But most would agree that there is something peculiar (wrong) about a system whose redistribution impact is in the opposite direction.

The plan Hansen and Weisbrod suggest for altering the pattern of higher-education subsidization to eliminate the regressive income redistributive effects of the present system is a distant cousin to the voucher plan for early schooling. Students are subsidized instead of schools, allowing for wider choice between public and private colleges. Grants are provided by a Higher Education Opportunity Program on a sliding scale to cover financing costs, with the size of the grant dwindling with the student's ability to pay out of his own, or his family's, resources.

The state schools would charge full-cost tuition. Hansen and Weisbrod argue that this plan would be more equitable, cheaper, and efficient than the present system. There is no disputing the first claim. Opportunity for college would be expanded for poorer students as the state financed not only their direct tuition costs but also their maintenance expenses.

According to Hansen and Weisbrod the plan would be cheaper than the present system because the state would now collect full-cost tuition from those able to pay. But they tend to underestimate student costs that would need to be subsidized. They use a figure of $2,100 per year comprised of tuition ($1,400), books ($100), and maintenance ($600). State schools tend to use instructional costs as their basis for calculating costs, omitting building expenses. One can wonder why private colleges in the same state charge $3,000 per year and still fall short of covering all costs with tuition. $600 per academic year, or $75 per month,

[7]W. Lee Hansen and Burton Weisbrod, "The Distribution of Costs and Direct Benefits of Public Higher Education: The Case of California," *Journal of Human Resources,* vol. 4, Spring 1969.

seems to be a figure taken from the 1940s to represent room, board, and incidental expenses.

As for efficiency changes under the plan, it is true that the present system of high equal subsidies does tend to lead to public overinvestment in, and excessive demand for, education because of the high private rate that can be earned by the individual student. But in reality the plan substitutes another form of inefficiency. With differential individual costs under the sliding-grant system, there would be greater investment among low-income than high-income students of the same ability (later earning capacity) and, what is more important, differential marginal rates of return and investment in education, a situation that precludes maximum investment efficiency.

SUMMARY

Although college financing needs may be only half as great as investment costs, they still form an imposing barrier to college attendance for many promising students. Apart from improving efficiency by allowing college investment for those who could earn a high return on their schooling, special funding plans would help alleviate poverty by improving college participation of the poor who would thereby increase their earnings potential.

A straight loan program, though, which provided funds at market interest rates would do nothing to improve the economic status of the poor who had to borrow all their investment costs and who earned only average rates of return on their educational investment. Outright grants would certainly help, but would be costly; give preference to education over other forms of income-generating investment; and might be an inefficient means of transferring income to the poor.

A combined grant-loan program, with the equity feature of repayments tied to later earnings, seems the most promising financing plan. With grants and loans reduced with ability of the student to finance his own college costs, retained earnings would be higher for those who contributed the most from their own resources; educational opportunity would be expanded, and the distorting feature of fixed loan plans with high repayments for those who profited little from college would be eliminated.

The current benefit-cost pattern for public higher education favors high-income students. A plan with full-cost tuition and subsidies declining with ability to pay would redistribute benefits toward low-income groups. But if true full-cost tuition were charged, the differential subsidy program might become expensive. On the one hand efficiency would be enhanced as some students bore the full cost of their investment, but on the other hand there would be a tendency for overinvestment (low rates of return) for heavily subsidized students.

All plans for educational financing reform—elimination of the property tax as the basis for early education funding, grant-loan-equity programs for higher education, proposals for changes in public college subsidies—are in the formative stages, untested and inchoate. They represent our gropings toward greater equity and efficiency in our rapidly expanding, most important, segment of human capital formation—investment in education.